Exploring the Cultural, Ideological and Economic Legacies of Euro 2012

European National football came together in the summer of 2012 for the 14th occasion. This book sets out to examine the enduring social tensions between supporters and authorities, as well as those between local, national and European identities, which formed the backdrop to the 14th staging of the European National football tournament, Euro 2012. The context of the tournament was somewhat unique from those staged in previous years, being jointly hosted for the first time by two post-Communist nations still in the process of social and economic transition. In this respect, the decision to stage Euro 2012 in Poland and Ukraine bore its own material and symbolic legacies shaping the tournament: the unsettling of neo-liberal imaginings and emergent 'East-West' fears about poor infrastructure, inefficiencies and corruption jostled with moral panics about racism and fears surrounding the potentially unfulfilled consumerist expectations of west European supporters.

The book seeks to explore the ideologies and practices invoked by competing national sentiments and examine the social tensions, ambiguities and social capital generating potentials surrounding national, ethnic, European identity, with respect to national football teams, supporters and supporter movements.

This book was originally published as a special issue of *Soccer & Society*.

Peter Kennedy lectures in the Sociology of Sports at Glasgow Caledonian University. His most recent published work is in applying sociological perspectives to understand the complex relationship between football clubs and fan culture.

Christos Kassimeris is Associate Professor in Political Science and heads the Department of Social and Behavioral Sciences at European University Cyprus. He is the author of *European Football in Black and White: Tackling Racism in Football*, editor of *Anti-Racism in European Football: Fair Play for All* and has published in journals such as *Soccer & Society* and *Sport in Society*. He is also Visiting Research Fellow at the International Centre for Sports History and Culture at De Montfort University.

Exploring the Cultural, Ideological and Economic Legacies of Euro 2012

Edited by
Peter Kennedy and Christos Kassimeris

Routledge
Taylor & Francis Group

LONDON AND NEW YORK

First published 2015 by Routledge

2 Park Square, Milton Park, Abingdon, Oxon OX14 4RN
711 Third Avenue, New York, NY 10017, USA

Routledge is an imprint of the Taylor & Francis Group, an informa business

First issued in paperback 2017

British Library Cataloguing in Publication Data
A catalogue record for this book is available from the British Library

ISBN 13: 978-1-138-81173-7 (hbk)
ISBN 13: 978-1-138-05815-6 (pbk)

Typeset in Times New Roman
by RefineCatch Limited, Bungay, Suffolk

Publisher's Note
The publisher accepts responsibility for any inconsistencies that may have
arisen during the conversion of this book from journal articles to book chapters,
namely the possible inclusion of journal terminology.

Disclaimer
Every effort has been made to contact copyright holders for their permission to
reprint material in this book. The publishers would be grateful to hear from any
copyright holder who is not here acknowledged and will undertake to rectify
any errors or omissions in future editions of this book.

Sport in the Global Society – Contemporary Perspectives
Series Editor: Boria Majumdar

The social, cultural (including media) and political study of sport is an expanding area of scholarship and related research. While this area has been well served by the *Sport in the Global Society* series, the surge in quality scholarship over the last few years has necessitated the creation of *Sport in the Global Society: Contemporary Perspectives*. The series will publish the work of leading scholars in fields as diverse as sociology, cultural studies, media studies, gender studies, cultural geography and history, political science and political economy. If the social and cultural study of sport is to receive the scholarly attention and readership it warrants, a cross-disciplinary series dedicated to taking sport beyond the narrow confines of physical education and sport science academic domains is necessary. *Sport in the Global Society: Contemporary Perspectives* will answer this need.

Titles in the Series

Contents

Citation Information

The chapters in this book were originally published in *Soccer & Society*, volume 15, issue 2 (March 2014). When citing this material, please use the original page numbering for each article, as follows:

Chapter 1
Introduction
Christos Kassimeris and Peter Kennedy
Soccer & Society, volume 15, issue 2 (March 2014) pp. 177–189

Chapter 2
The Semiotics of European Football
Christos Kassimeris
Soccer & Society, volume 15, issue 2 (March 2014) pp. 190–202

Chapter 3
Playing with tension: national charisma and disgrace at Euro 2012
Alex Law
Soccer & Society, volume 15, issue 2 (March 2014) pp. 203–221

Chapter 4
'They think it's all Dover!' Popular newspaper narratives and images about the English football team and (re)presentations of national identity during Euro 2012
John Vincent and John Harris
Soccer & Society, volume 15, issue 2 (March 2014) pp. 222–240

Chapter 5
German football culture in the new millennium: ethnic diversity, flair and youth on and off the pitch
Udo Merkel
Soccer & Society, volume 15, issue 2 (March 2014) pp. 241–255

Chapter 6
Poles apart: foreign players, Polish football and Euro 2012
Richard Elliott and Konrad Bania
Soccer & Society, volume 15, issue 2 (March 2014) pp. 256–271

Chapter 7

"Sometimes you go into competitions with little or no expectations": England, Euro 2012 in the context of austerity
Peter Kennedy
Soccer & Society, volume 15, issue 2 (March 2014) pp. 272–289

Please direct any queries you may have about the citations to
clsuk.permissions@cengage.com

INTRODUCTION

Christos Kassimeris[a] and Peter Kennedy[b]

[a]Department of Social & Behavioural Sciences, European University Cyprus, Nicosia, Cyprus;
[b]Glasgow Caledonian University, Glasgow, UK

The 14th European Football Championships (Euro 2012) was held between 8 June and 2 July 2012, hosted jointly by Poland and Ukraine, the first ex-Soviet bloc countries to host the final stages of this tournament. This special issue of *Soccer and Society* brings together a range of prominent authors to reflect on the event itself and its wider social, cultural and political consequences. This introduction set the scene. Firstly, by reflecting on the tournaments origins as a cold war Legacy and how 'legacy', interpreted dialectically (active across past, present and future), illuminates an understanding of the recent Euro 2012. And secondly, by introducing each author's contribution to this special issue. The Euros are the culmination of the interweaving of the national and the local across time, linked by the cultural threads of imperial expansion. The Euros are also evidence manifest that the origins of football, although driven by imperial expansion of trade and labour power, are truly European. Therefore, before we go any further, it is worth reflecting on the Europeanization of football, as its movement and development weave together the national and the local.

The Europeanization of football

Organized by the English, and soon after it was introduced to the rest of the United Kingdom, football travelled across continental Europe effortlessly, reaching first those countries that geographically surround Britain. It first visited Denmark where Kjobenhavns Boldklub was founded in the capital of Copenhagen by some Englishmen as early as 1876, thus becoming the oldest European club outside Britain, followed by the setting up of the Danish Football Association (est. 1889) and the commencement of a league in 1915. In nearby Sweden, it was Scotsmen who introduced football to the city of Gothenburg founding Lyckans Soldater and Örgryte IS in 1883 and 1887, respectively, with the same two playing the first football match ever recorded in 1892. The first Dutch football club was Haarlemse founded in 1879 by Pim Mulier, a Dutchman educated in England. As a matter of fact, football's English influence was strong in the Netherlands too, with English textile workers introducing the game to the Dutch. While some clubs retain their English names today – Be Quick in Gronigen and Go Ahead in Deventer – it is important to note that the names of some other clubs, such as Ajax and Hercules, have their origins in classical Greece, founded by students majoring in relevant studies. Still across the

English shores, Le Havre was the oldest French football club, founded by either sailors or students from Britain, since the game of football was first introduced to the west coast of France.

The expansion of football over Central Europe was no different. Football in Germany too was influenced by the local British population and visiting British students. The first club to test the waters in a gymnastics-dominated Germany, the Anglo-American Football Club, was founded in 1881 (renamed Hamburg in 1897), followed by Hertha Berlin in 1892. Interestingly, the first recorded football game in Germany was contested in 1896 by the very same two clubs, with a national league kicking off in 1902. In Bohemia, what is today Czech Republic, Athletic Club King's Vineyard (renamed Sparta Prague soon after) and Slavia Prague–the classic Prague duo – were established in 1892 and 1893, respectively. The first league was set up in 1896, but was limited to the clubs based in and around Prague due to the fact that Bohemia was part of the Austro-Hungarian Empire. Likewise, football in Poland was first introduced to Krakow because of the lenient attitude of the House of Habsburgs towards the Poles, much unlike the case regarding the rest of the Polish nation that was under the rule of the German and Russian Empires. The first Polish clubs were KS Cracovia and Wisła Kraków SSA, whereas football clubs would emerge from the Russian section a few years later as the city of Lodz witnessed the birth of ŁKS Łódź and RTS WidzewŁódź. Further to the east, Orekhovo Sports Club was founded in Russia in 1887 by Clement and Harry Charnock, two English brothers involved in the textile business, both supporters of Blackburn Rovers Football Club. Today, the club is known as Dinamo Moscow, renamed after the Russian Revolution of 1917, and continues to play in Blackburn's blue and white colours. However, it appears that football was more widely played in 1890 among the Englishmen of St. Petersburg.

In Mediterranean Italy, Genoa Cricket and Football Club was founded in 1893 by British sailors and tradesmen. James Richardson Spensely is considered to be the founder of the club that was made up by English players, as no Italians were allowed before 1897. The year after, Athletic Bilbao was founded much because of the close cooperation between English and Basques. The influence of the English becomes evident in that the club continues to play in the red-and-white strips of Sunderland Football Club. Nonetheless, Spain's first football club actually is Recreativo Huelva, an all – Spanish side that was founded in 1889. In the other Iberian nation, Portugal, Lisbon was founded in 1875 by British sailors, while Boavista's Footballers – later renamed Boavista – was founded by British entrepreneurs and Portuguese textile workers in 1903. Finally, in Greece, English bankers set up the first club in Athens, a club originally known as Panhellenic, renamed Panathinaikos in 1908. In neighbouring Yugoslavia, what is probably the first local football club, HNK Hajduk Split, was named after the *hajduks* that resisted the Ottoman Turks. Similarly, nationalistic was the 'HNK', which stands for Hrvatski Nogometni Klub, or else 'Croatian Football Club.'

All pioneers in European club football, their British heritage undoubtedly momentous, some of the clubs mentioned above not only continue to exist but have also claimed much success over the years. These clubs led by example and helped nurture football at both local and national level to an extent where, nowadays, some five hundred thousand football clubs are officially registered with their national football associations. Simply put, there is hardly a community of any kind in Europe that is not represented in football–that much popular is the game.

European football competitions

The competitive nature of the game of football made certain that sporting rivalries would soon emerge, at least at local level, which brought about a rather festive atmosphere during those early matches in particular. Not surprisingly, the popularity that football had gained in the pre-war period was the catalyst that provided the necessary grounds for the first continental competition.

Gabriel Hanot, a French journalist for L'Equipe, presented in 1954 his ideas about a football competition where the champions of Europe's national leagues would come to compete in a pan-European league. The majority of Europe's top football clubs responded with much enthusiasm, since the prospect of claiming a European championship was difficult to resist, yet the idea of setting up a league that would have to have a considerable number of fixtures was deemed problematic at the time. Instead, clubs seemed to favour a European football competition that resembled much how cup competitions were organized at national level, therefore, prompting L'Equipe to invite on January 1955, 18 clubs to enter the first such cup competition, the European Cup. It is noteworthy that not all invited clubs were champions at home; some were preferred over the actual winners of certain domestic leagues simply because of their appeal to the fans.

What this football competition made obvious, nevertheless, was the need for an independent body to organize the competition, mediate between clubs when necessary and, most importantly, oversee the implementation of the relevant policies and regulations. That organization was, of course, the Union of European Football Associations (UEFA), which, although established a year earlier, had a rather ambiguous role in European football. As soon as the European Cup witnessed success all over the continent, what seemed like an organization that served little purpose immediately gained immense prestige. In an attempt to defend the competition from the influence that was the Cold War division of Europe, UEFA moved their headquarters from France to Switzerland in 1960, so as to make good use of the country's geographic location, ideological neutrality, political stability and economic prosperity.

The UEFA Cup, previously known as the Inter-Cities Fair Cup (since it was originally open to clubs coming from cities that hosted trade fairs), closely followed the apparent success of the European Cup. The success of both football competitions encouraged UEFA to set up yet another football competition, the European Cup-Winners' Cup. The Cup-Winners' Cup was first contested in 1960 and was open to clubs that had won their domestic cup competition. Needless to say, the European Cup-Winners' Cup too witnessed considerable success. The impact of all three football competitions and their overall contribution to promoting European football was certainly fundamental, considering that they all allowed UEFA to foster more interaction among Europe's leading football clubs and, of course, more football mobility around the continent.

All the while, European club football was gaining unparalleled popularity, the secretary of the French Football Federation, Henri Delaunay, proposed in the mid-1950s a competition that would in essence bring together regional tournaments such as the British Home Championship, the Mitropa Cup and the Nordic Cup, in order to promote football competition at national level as well. In its early days, the competition included home and away matches, however, the semi-finals and final took place in one single country. Of the 33 European national football associations of the time, 17 entered the first competition that was named the European Nations Cup.

The British nations, Italy, Sweden and West Germany, among others, decided not to participate for they considered such a continental competition entirely meaningless. In the preliminary round that was held on 5 April 1958, in order to allow the more manageable 16 nations to compete for the first ever European Nations Cup, Czechoslovakia beat the Republic of Ireland to pave the way to the first ever pan-European tournament that was won by the Soviet Union in Paris. Today known as European Championship, or else Euro, association football continues to excite football fans around Europe, particularly, when the so-called 'underdogs' such as Denmark in 1992 and Greece in 2004 succeed in disturbing the waters by winning the competition. Interestingly, none of the British nations, where football was first organized and developed, has ever reached the final.

The Euros across East and West

The choice of Poland and Ukraine to host Euro 2012 came as a surprise to many. Italy seemed clear favourites (despite emerging issues such as on-going investigations into 'wide scale match-fixing scandal in Serie A' and 'the death of policeman when soccer fans rioted in Catania').[1] From UEFA's perspective, the choice served as a reminder of the wider European project to which it aspires (an aspiration also manifest in the recent decision by UEFA to extend the finals to 24 nations to be pan-hosted by nations across Europe). For UEFA, the Euros and UEFA itself, have come full circle from the post-1945 cold war climate of East vs. West and the attempt by FIFA and the newly formed UEFA (1954) to use the popularity of football to do its bit to assist in generating a sense of European unity across East and West.

Initially, UEFA's aspirations for a wider European unity looked good on paper, but met resistance from the realpolitik of the global cold war era and many might argue that it became part of the 'soft power' of 'war by other means' fought out by divided powers. Nevertheless, UEFA's aspirations towards Europe developed during the 1970s, due largely to the wider détente between the US and the USSR, which allowed some thawing in the political posturing between nations East and West of the 'iron curtain'. This encouraged an extension of the original format of four nation's finals into a tournament of eight nations, a format recognizable to the modern audience. If we measure success on the field in terms of reaching the finals, then, in the early decades of the tournament at least, nations from the East European Bloc matched the success of those in the Capitalist West, by reaching the final of the first five tournaments held between 1960 and 1976. Since then, reflecting, in part, the disintegration of the Soviet Union, the balance of success has shifted away from East European nations, as three nations have come to dominate the tournament – Germany, Spain and France – winning between them 8 of the 14 tournaments staged.

Euro 2012

In the month building up to Euro 2012, the West European media painted a grim picture of the event to come, highlighting potential tournament boycotts from fans in the West, concerned about travel and tourist restrictions and by French and English officials protesting at the imprisonment of former Premier Yulia Tymoshenko on charges of corruption. The added moral panics concerning racist and xenophobic fans, further spurred on the negative press in the lead up to the tournament. Ukraine was thought to be 'staring at nothing less than a full-blown PR disaster'[2] over tourist profiteering and its treatment of Tymoshenko, while concerns abounded about secret right-wing training camps have been filmed taking place outside Kiev as 'Patriots' prepare for the 'war against immigrants'.[3]

Yet, despite the negative press, both real and imagined, Euro 2012 defied predictions and turned out to be a successful tournament on its own terms. More supporters than ever before attended live matches. Indeed, Euro 2012 demonstrated once again football's recession-proof credentials by hosting an event that outstripped Euro 2008. Globally just over one billion television viewers watched Euro 2008, 1.1 million spectators attended live matches and 4.2 million attended 'fan zones'.[4] Euro 2012 outperformed in every area: 1.6 billion television viewers watched Euro 2012, while 1.4 million and 7 million fans attended live matches and fan zones, respectively.[5] Republicans will also be heartened to know that the average per match viewing figure of 150 million surpassed figures for both Prince William's wedding to Kate Middleton in 2011 and Queen Elizabeth II's jubilee concert in June 2012.[6]

Matches proved to be highly competitive, exciting and high-quality contests. The football geek within may be interested to know that the after-tournament technical appraisal of the games carried out by UEFA had discovered the development of a new playing style, less enthralled by the long ball and counter-attack and more prone towards chess-like flexible use of fullback and wingers to by-pass the wall of central defenders (buttressed by meddlesome defensive midfielders)[7] jamming up the middle of the pitch. Ironically, despite the constant chatter from pundits about this emerging passing, pressing, possession game, played by strikerless teams, populated by low centre of gravity artists (keen to walk the ball into the net), just short of a third of all goals were scored with the head from well-angled crosses or set play:[8] so much for the 'short ball revolution'.

In terms of hard cash, Euro 2012 has more than delivered, generating a total commercial revenue of €1.345 billion[9] (a slight increase on Euro2008 revenue, but 50% more than Euro 2004). The chart below gives a clear indication of the torrent of capital that has poured into each successive Euro finals between 1996 and 2008.

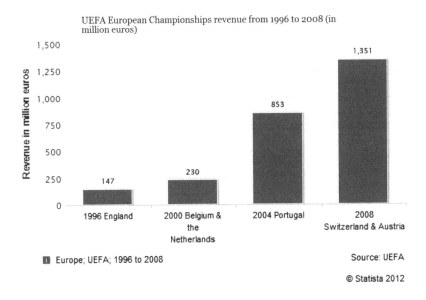

UEFA European Championships revenue from 1996 to 2008 (in million euros)

Europe; UEFA; 1996 to 2008

Source: UEFA

© Statista 2012

Too early to talk legacies?

The above headline figures appear very impressive indeed, but what can be sensibly inferred from them about 'legacy'? Over recent decades, mega sporting events such as the Euros have become the object and subject of various 'legacy' discourses often put forward by social groups keen to achieve closure over the meaning of 'legacy' for more 'practical' purposes. Those bodies charged with hosting sporting events attempt *meaning closure* over 'legacy' around perceived partnerships, imagined communities of shared interests, pursuing (apparently agreed upon) economic, social and cultural benefits for the good of all involved. The simple definition of legacy, 'what gets left behind after a major sporting event', is both narrow and relatively straightforward, but encompasses a wide range of content, wide enough to make the 'known known' as well as 'unknown' to echo Horne.[10] Holger has helpfully reviewed the list of positive and negative content in the 'known' literature:

> Examples range from commonly recognised aspects (urban planning, sport infrastructure) to less recognised intangible legacies such as urban regeneration, enhanced international reputation, increased tourism, improved public welfare, additional employment, more local business opportunities, better corporate relocation, opportunities for city marketing, renewed community spirit, better inter-regional cooperation, production of ideas, production of cultural values, popular memory, opportunities for education, emotional experience and additional know-how. These positive legacies stand in contrast to negative legacies such as debts from construction, high opportunity costs, unneeded infrastructure, temporary crowding-out, loss of permanently returning tourists, increases of property rental, socially unjust displacement and re-distributions.[11]

Here, both positive and negative contents are listed. Horne, as indicated above and in relation to sport, writes of 'unknown knowns', things that we 'knew' but have forgotten.[12] Without undue damage to the original meaning, this could be reversed to understand legacy discourses in terms of 'knowns and unknowns'. In this respect, the content listed in the quote above indicates 'known knowns', things we know we know and are familiar with in legacy-speak. The list also offers a glimpse of certain 'known unknowns' too; things we are aware of but treat as 'unknowns' with respect to the impact they exert on our present and future practice.

Taking account of the dialectic between 'known and unknowns', leads one to acknowledge that positive and negative contents of 'legacy' may not be so easily separated; what is positive and negative with respect to legacy building is in the eye of the beholding group interest rather than in some mythical unity of interests. For example, large contractors build sport infrastructure as part of a major sport event in the belief that it will turn a handsome profit and the local state in the belief that it will be beneficial to the community (the contractor's and local stat's 'positive leg-acy'), while the collective wisdom of society (the source of the 'known' 'unknown') reveals this to be 'unneeded infrastructure' at 'high opportunity costs' for the host community (the communities 'negative legacy').

Previous Euro tournaments demonstrate this dialectic. Portugal 2004 created employment opportunities (positive legacy) but mainly low-waged and short-term, hence sustain the category of under-employment (negative legacy); some excellent stadiums were created (positive legacy) but stadiums with high opportunity costs to the community and unlikely to be filled each week (negative legacy). We 'know' this because it is part of the legacy left behind by our previous claims and counter claims about legacies, which some literature tends to forget, as the next bandwagon for new mega event opportunities hits town.

East–West legacies active in the creation of 'Euro 2012'

As the above intimates, the dominant approach to 'legacy' is to see it as 'the legacy going forward'; the *predicted impact* an event will have for the economy, community, etc. of the sporting mega-event ('measurable' as 'units' of economic, cultural and social capital). However, while debates about the meanings and consequences of sporting legacies continue, we should also bear in mind that mega sporting events like the Euro 2012 are the product of legacies. Accordingly, instead of only asking what will be this or that sporting events' legacy, one ought also to ask what legacies have come together in such a way to produce *this* sporting mega event *now* in this way and not in some other way. Talk about Mega sporting event legacies rarely focus on this, they tend to be abstracted from their historically specific social structural relations (*their own legacy*).

Euro 2012 has its own legacy: East–West Legacies are active in creating 'Euro 2012'. One is global austerity and the other is Stalinism. The issue of austerity loomed large economically but also permeated the tournament itself. Much of the press reportage appeared to confirm the historic debate within critical theory over the dialectical relation between economics and culture, or how wider economic troubles find their way in to sport, sometimes as reflection sometimes as deflection. One reflection was in the close attention paid to player accommodation and its appropriateness to austere times. The Portuguese press, for example, raised the complaint that 'The squad's arrangements for Euro 2012 are too lavish for the austerity-hit country'.[13] Others revealed a preoccupation with austerity as a style of play to win matches. Recalling Chelsea's austere performance in defeating first Barcelona and then Bayern Munich to lift the Champions League title in May 2012 (winning without the ball), a way forward for England were announced by the following headline, 'Euro 2012: Austerity Measures Represent England's Best Chance of Success'.[14] To quote the heading of one broadsheet newspaper, 'blue Peter-style opening ceremony spot on in its brevity and austerity'.[15]

There was plenty of evidence of the deflector capacity of sport too, as the following response to Greece's 1–0 win over Russia, which leapfrogged them above Russia into the play-off stages,

> For Greeks who have seen their living standards plummet in the debt crisis, their team's unexpected win against Russia on Saturday night was as much about national validation as sporting prowess. Street celebrations in Athens saw Greeks wrapped in their flag, wearing replica helmets of ancient Greek warriors and waving spears.[16]

The political economic legacy of Euro 2012 is also the outcome of the scars of Stalinism, manifest in discourses of inefficiency, corruption, xenophobia; the seductions of neo-liberal ideals, manifest in discourses of commodification, urban renewal and place branding related to sport. Each of these played their part in the creation 'Euro 2012'. The legacy of Stalinism is manifest in the scale of investment, 40× more capital investment that Euro 2008 and 10× more than Euro 2004, the latter devoted mostly to new stadium builds.[17] The event provided an occasion for the host nations to attempt to modernize road, rail, airport tourist and business infrastructure on a grand scale. Ninty percent of the €38 billion capital investment spent on the latter dwarfed the 10% allocated to Stadium modernization.[18] However, the aim to develop infrastructure up to the expectations of the EU came up against the realities of a post-Soviet business environment. Not all the projects were constructed on time and some remain unfinished and job creation although significant in both nations were mostly temporary and low paid. The return from tourism and foreign direct investment is unlikely to cover even a fraction of the €38 billion outlay, leading to increased public debt in both Ukraine and Poland and adding to problems servicing this debt through the global financial markets. The latter compounded by allegations that, 'UEFA, the governing body of football in Europe, is under pressure to investigate claims of massive corruption during Ukraine's preparations for Euro 2012, amid allegations that as much as $4bn (£2.5bn) in state funds allocated for the tournament was stolen by officials'.[19]

In summary, the decision to stage Euro 2012 in Poland and Ukraine has borne its own material and symbolic legacies shaping the tournament we construct: the unsettling of neoliberal imaginings and emergent 'East–West' fears about poor infrastructure, inefficiencies and corruption jostled with moral panics about racism and fears surrounding the potentially unfulfilled consumerist expectations of west European supporters. They cannot be ignored because they are the sporting legacy leading up to Euro 2012. Nevertheless, the occasion itself, how it develops, what it brings to light, the sense of euphoria, hope and despair it carries with it are the outcome not only of the past, but also of the event itself. Past and present come together in shaping the actual event, determining the legacy it will bring to bear in the future. As we now go on to consider, it is this sense of the importance of past and present, which establishes the agenda for the contributions to this special issue.

Contributors

The paper by Kassimeris reflects on the symbolic importance of emblems adorning the national football teams at the Euros, draws links between sport and war in the process. As Kassimeris reflects,

> like any other identity, national identity has to be learnt. Important instruments in any learning process are various kinds of audio-visual aids, and so also in the school of national identity construction. That is why national symbols – flags, coats of arms, national anthems – play such a crucial role in nation building and nation-maintenance.

Perhaps know here is this more clearly articulated than in and through football. In demonstrating this, Kassimeris studies the origins of the emblems representing the sixteen national football associations and the respective teams that contested for European glory in the stadiums of Poland and Ukraine. In a detailed account, he describes how these emblems decorate the shirts of football players, often denoting uncommon symbolic significance, while also conveying copious amounts of historical and cultural information that command academic attention. Moreover, Kassimeris uncovers interesting regional unities in the display and meaning of emblems, between Southern and Eastern and between Northern and Western European nations, which clearly document the period of history during which they came into being and important aspects of their culture. Given the overwhelming symbolic import of coats of arms is a marked feature of Kassimeris' study, leading him to reflect that the very same banners that once headed the advance of European armies today lead national football teams. Further confirming the close links between the development of sport and militarization in the formation of national identity.

Sporting competitions have long been understood as analogous to war by other means and part of the sports mode of production specific to capitalism. Law's contribution to this special edition argues that major football events such as Euro 2012 offer themselves as occasions for the working out of national tensions against the backdrop of weakly formed regional identities and broader historical forces shaping and influencing the present. In particular, the Euros need to be understood against the backdrop of Europeanization unification process, which remain in a state of flux and uncertainty at the time of global recession and inter-state rivalries. Resurgent national competition, aggression and tensions throughout Europe provided the context for Euro 2012. Law's paper addresses the crucial question of what role do major sport events have in such contexts? In addressing this question, Law considers aspects of the explanatory powers of two opposing theoretical perspectives, Hyper-Critical Theory' and key elements of figurational theory arising from the work of Elias and Dunning. On the one hand, Hyper-Critical Theory would predict that the potential for national aggression, competition and tensions inherent to sports events such as the Euros, would echo and amplify the all too real aggressions and fierce competitive rivalries within the wider capitalist political economy between nation-states struggling to export the worst of the negative consequences of austerity to others. On the other hand, Elias and Dunning's theory, which places emphasis on the mimetic and displacement value of sport for managing violence and national enmity through controlled cathartic, would predict that the Euros would reflect, but also deflect, dissipate and becalm national rivalries. Reflecting on his findings drawn from the data derived from Euronews coverage of Euro 2012, Law argues that, contra to the claims of Hyper-Critical Theory, 'Euro 2012 is one of the few collective events that fosters a cross-national figuration rather than simply furthering the interests of commercialized sport and militarism anticipated by Hyper-Critical Theory'. Law concludes that 'Hyper-Critical Theory has effectively abandoned the utopian moment of the repressed desires that football figurations like Euro 2012 expresses'.

The English national football team in the finals of a major tournament are usually more than enough ingredients for media reconstructions of national identities premised on the twin victories of World War II and World Cup 66 to counter the ebbing away of the waves 'Britannia' once claimed to rule over. The context of Euro 2012 added a few more ingredients which presented an imaginative challenge to the traditional role of the media in 'shaping, (re)producing and reflecting a shared national cultural consciousness' in ways other than a regression to mythical golden eras. However, in times of economic turbulence across Europe, a crisis in the EU currency regime, the Queen Elizabeth II Jubilee celebrations, London Olympics on the near horizon and the not so distant echoes of social unrest throughout the UK in the summer of 2011, mythical pasts often look all the rosier in seeking out national identities. The authors make use of Guibernau articulation of media power to frame media representations of English identities. Drawing out analysis of the two most popular 'red tops' in England, *The Daily Mirror* and the *Daily Sun*, the authors illustrate how the media succumb all to easily to a 'wilful nostalgia' based on tried and tested formulae to resurrect for present consumption of mono-ethnic tales of glory days, of stiff upper lips defending 'empire', of selfless bravery in the face of adversity and of never-ending never say die attitudes. Euro 2012 is no exception to previous major tournaments in offering an occasion for ignoring the countries' general decline and projecting out-dated mythologies.

One of the most striking features of recent national football tournaments is the stark change in the German football teams' style of play, lauded as much these days for its flair and creativity, as much as its athleticism and efficiency. Merkel's paper links this transformation in style to the ethnic and cultural diversity of the German national side, which took to the field at Euro 2012 and is the product of a new sense of national identity within contemporary German society, manifest in widespread and colourful celebrations of a new, modern sense of Germanness underpinned by a non-threatening and playful patriotism. The origins of the spread and popularity of football in Germany lay in the waves of immigration into Germany during the twentieth century. In 1920, working class Polish immigration to Germany drawn together under conditions of rapid industrial expansion in the Rhineland and Westphalia into enclaves in response to social exclusion. Football was their national game and a source of collective identity and status. For decades after, Germany would continue to respond negatively to immigration and the national team became symbolic of a deeply conservative stance on national identity – for 'real' Germans only! The second wave of immigration, this time from Turkey decades later, coupled with the gradual detachment of club football from local ties and more generally the commercialization of sport, all served to melt the conservative attitude to immigrants and allow to flourish a new multicultural attitude amongst the wider population. Organizers of the national football team, spurred on by the latter as well as by failure on the field of play at Euro 2000, began to experiment with new styles of youth coaching and embrace a new sense of identity more inclusive of different ethnicities. The multicultural biographies of members of the German national side at Euro 2012 are testimony to these broader social changes. As Merkel reflects, 'the composition of the German side that played Turkey in 2010 and, later, competed in Euro 2012 offers more valuable insights into the more embracing attitude of Germans and the redefined sense of Germanness in the twenty-first century'.

Elliot and Bania use the occasion of Euro 2012 to examine the various push and pull factors influencing the flow of football players into Poland's top league, the Ekstraklasa. Elite professional football players traditionally flow to the core nations in Europe – England, Germany, Spain, France and Italy, reflecting the uneven but fluid nature of globalization across core and periphery. However, as the authors point out, the European Football Championship and the World Cup have been used recently to assist periphery nations with aspirations of moving closer to the core, by offering opportunities to hosting major events. Poland's co-hosting of Euro 2012 provides such opportunities, via the hoped for capital injection, the attraction of new fans and exposure to global media. Against this background, Elliot and Bania present findings from their research on factors driving the inward flow of footballers into the Ekstraklasa, a league in transition between core and periphery status in the European pecking order. Focusing on the insights of football players, drawn from interview data, the authors found that player's decisions to migrate to Poland to play football, while unsurprisingly complex and idiosyncratic to the individual concerned, were influenced more broadly by push factors, the positive salary disparity between Poland and country of origin; and pull factors, the opportunities the move opened up to play in the European Champions League and the Europa Cup competitions. The Ekstraklas was in this respect a stepping stone in a double sense: players hoping to progress to a higher level of football migrated to a league in a nation with its own ambitions to progress closer to the core of European football nations. Hosting the 2012 European Championships, argue Elliot and Bania, is something of a watershed in rebalancing the state of 'dependent-development' vis-à-vis the Western core and in providing a global platform for Poland to market employment opportunities available in the Ekstraklasa.

Kennedy's paper analyses media coverage of the England football team in the run up to Euro 2012. He describes how the dominant discourse of 'low expectations' underpinned media representations of England and considers various reasons for this, including the resignation and replacement of England managers prior to the tournament, the intra-team tensions arising from racism, along with longer term factors, including the perceived constraints placed on the England national team's development by the English Premier League. While all of these factors are important, Kennedy suggests that they cannot alone, or even in combination, sufficiently explain why the discourse of 'low expectations' took such a hold over media representations of the England national team. He argues that one missing factor is the broader problems facing the economy and society, particularly the national and supra-national preoccupation with 'austerity', which has created an aura of low expectations and a somewhat perverse way of dealing with austerity; particularly the tendency to represent 'austerity' *as* 'growth' in a 'low expectations' culture. Previous research has demonstrated the links between the fortunes of the wider economy and sentiments surrounding the fate of the English national team. In his paper, Kennedy takes the opportunity to reconsider these wider links in terms of an *elective affinity*, arguing that the discourse of 'low expectations' haunting the England team in the present period is the manifestation and transference of a more pervasive general lowering of expectations amongst the media and the political elite, concerning the present and future political economic prospects of economic growth and social prosperity. He argues that the elective affinity between the new realism of low expectations within the wider political and cultural economy offers a wider context for understanding the language of low expectations saturating media narration of England's fate prior to and during the Euros.

When two football teams face each other in the theatre of dreams, they are far from the only determinants in the making of the drama unfolding. Referee and their officials play their part. Refereeing is the game within the game, a demonstration of the art of orchestration and control, the pitch an arena where they can demonstrate their own skills and impose their own philosophies towards that 'other' game. At one and the same time, 'guardians', 'enforcers', 'authoritarian's', 'mediators' and 'legislators', officials are praised for letting the game flow, and admonished for ignoring the 'foul' tackle; the official's game is forever the subject of critical scrutiny.

Notes

1. *The Independent*. 'Poland and Ukraine to Co-host Euro 2012'.
2. *The Guardian*. 'Euro 2012 Turning into PR Disaster for Ukraine as Racism Fears Scare off Fans'.
3. *MailOnline*. May 2012.
4. World Intellectual Property Organisation. 'EUFA's Battle for its Brand', April 2012.
5. UEFA.com. 'Polish Pride at EURO Success', July 2012.
6. *EU business*. 'Football: UEFA Hails "Exceptional" Euro 2012 for TV, Media', June 2012.
7. UEFA, *Technical Report* (Genève: UEFA).
8. UEFA, *Technical Report* (Genève: UEFA).
9. *Arab News*. 'UEFA Expects 250M Viewers for Euro Final', June 2012.
10. J. Horne, 'The Four "Knowns" of Sports Mega-events', *Leisure Studies* 26, no. 1: 81–96.
11. P. Holger, 'The Conceptualisation and Measurement of Mega Sport Event Legacies'.
12. J. Horne, 'The Four "Knowns" of Sports Mega-events'.
13. *The Independent*. 'Portugal's Austerity Fears Taken for a Ride by National Team's Euro 2012 Arrangements'.
14. *The Huffington Post*. 'Euro 2012: Austerity Measures Represent England's Best Chance of Success', June 2012.
15. *The Telegraph*. 'Euro 2012: Blue Peter-style Opening Ceremony Spot on in its Brevity and Austerity'.
16. *Okespanol*. 'Crisis, What Crisis? Euro 2012 Soccer Wins Bring Cheer to Europeans Struggling with Austerity'.
17. Euro 2012 Poland Ukraine. 'EURO 2012 Expenditure Broke the Record'.
18. EU Infrastructure. 'Poland and Ukraine to Spend Big on Euro'.
19. *The Guardian*. 'Euro 2012: UEFA Urged to Investigate $4bn Corruption Allegations in Ukraine'.

References

Arab News. 'UEFA Expects 250M Viewers for Euro Final', June 2012, http://www.arabnews.com/uefa-expects-250m-tv-audience-euro-2012-final.

EU business. 'Football: UEFA Hails "Exceptional" Euro 2012 for TV, Media' June 2012, http://www.eubusiness.com/news-eu/media-television.hjp/.

EU Infrastructure. 'Poland and Ukraine to Spend Big on Euro' 2012', September 2010, http://www.euinfrastructure.com/article/Poland-and-Ukraine-to-spend-big-on-Euro-2012/.

Euro 2012 Poland Ukraine. 'EURO 2012 Expenditure Broke the Record', August 2011, http://euro-2012news.com/analytics/590/euro-2012-expenditure-broke-the-record.

Holger, P. 'The Conceptualisation and Measurement of Mega Sport Event Legacies'. *Journal of Sport & Tourism* 12, no. 3–4 (2007): 207–28.

Horne, J. 'The Four "Knowns" of Sports Mega-events'. *Leisure Studies* 26, no. 1 (2007): 81–96.

MailOnline. May 2012. http://www.dailymail.co.uk/news/article-2150542/Nazi-mob-lies-wait-England-fans-Riot-police-march-battle-thugs-Euro-2012-terraces–turn-blind-eye-racist-chants-violence.html.

Okespanol. 'Crisis, What Crisis? Euro 2012 Soccer Wins Bring Cheer to Europeans Struggling with Austerity', June 2012, http://okespanol.com/crisis-what-crisis-euro-2012-soccer-wins-bring-cheer-to-europeans-struggling-with-austerity/.

The Guardian. 'Euro 2012 Turning into PR Disaster for Ukraine as Racism Fears Scare off Fans', May 2012, http://www.guardian.co.uk/football/2012/may/28/euro-2012-ukraine-sol-campbell.

The Guardian. 'Euro 2012: UEFA Urged to Investigate $4bn Corruption Allegations in Ukraine', June 2012, http://www.guardian.co.uk/football/2012/jun/20/euro-2012-corruption-allegations-ukraine.

The Huffington Post. 'Euro 2012: Austerity Measures Represent England's Best Chance of Success', June 2012, http://www.huffingtonpost.co.uk/james-hunt/euro-2012-austerity-measures-england_b_1567126.html.

The Independent. 'Poland and Ukraine to Co-host Euro 2012', April 2007, http://www. independent.co.uk/sport/football/european/poland-and-ukraine-to-cohost-euro-2012- 445263.html.

The Independent. 'Portugal's Austerity Fears Taken for a Ride by National Team's Euro 2012 Arrangements', June 2012, http://www.independent.co.uk/sport/football/international/ portugals-austerity-fears-taken-for-a-ride-by-national-teams-euro-2012-arrangements- 7827872.html.

The Telegraph. 'Euro 2012: Blue Peter-style Opening Ceremony Spot on in its Brevity and Austerity', June 2012, http://www.telegraph.co.uk/sport/football/competitions/euro-2012/ 9320529/Euro-2012-Blue-Peter-style-opening-ceremony-spot-on-in-its-brevity-and- austerity.html.

UEFA. *Technical Report.* Geneve: UEFA, 2012.

UEFA.com. 'Polish Pride at EURO Success', July 2012, http://uk.uefa.com/uefaeuro/news/ newsid=1841839.html.

World Intellectual Property Organisation. 'EUFA's Battle for its Brand', April 2012, http:// www.wipo.int/wipo_magazine/en/2012/02/article_0008.html.

The Semiotics of European Football

Christos Kassimeris

Department of Social & Behavioural Sciences, European University Cyprus, Nicosia, Cyprus

The present study concerns the origins of the emblems representing the sixteen national football associations and the respective teams that contested for European glory in the stadiums of Poland and Ukraine for it is of paramount significance, cultural and otherwise, to determine those explicit features that so expressively epitomize their sheer essence. These emblems decorate the shirts of football players, often denoting uncommon symbolic significance, while also conveying copious amounts of historical and cultural information that command academic attention.

The first international body to govern football was the *Fédération Internationale de Football Association* (FIFA). FIFA's foundation (1904) – when considered, of course, as an international event – occurred during what was a rather tumultuous period of time better known, perhaps, for the wars and revolutions that sustained the rise of the age of nationalism. Europe, in particular, was a continent destined for a violent eruption as nations competed for either hegemony or liberation. Debating the essence of nationalism or the definition of a nation within the context of a sports federation, therefore, would certainly seem inappropriate, unless the all-important subject of membership was in the balance. When Bohemia applied for membership with FIFA, whatever subtle definition of the term 'nation' was employed, it was obviously deemed too significant an issue for Austria to oppose its admission. At the time, Bohemia, or else modern-day Czech Republic, was an integral part of the Austro-Hungarian Empire and was, for that reason, considered ineligible for admission to an otherwise a political organization such as FIFA. Under similar conditions, Austria, with the support of Germany, formed a formidable stumbling block to the aspirations of Ireland, Scotland and Wales, as soon as they expressed an interest in joining football's world governing body. The two central European states' line of argument suggested that all three were part of the UK and thus not 'independent' enough to seek membership with an international organization.

The case of the UK serves us well. Indeed, 'sport can promote both the identity of national minorities as in the case of international football competitions and the collective British identity in the case of the Olympics where all nations together as one represent Britain. However, Ireland is indeed a complicated issue when considering that in rugby, for example, there is one team representing both Northern Ireland and the Republic of Ireland, whereas in the case of soccer they appear separated. The existence of national identities other than the English has differentiated the notion of

Englishness to that of British identity. During the World Cup finals in 1966, the English spectators were primarily waving the British flag, which is a mixture of Scottish, English and Welsh flags. When England won the 2003 World Rugby Cup, those flags promoting the notion of Britishness were replaced by the English flag, the red cross of St George'.[1] Evidently, the four national football teams representing England, Northern Ireland, Scotland and Wales, respectively, play a rather important role in both expressing independence, as well as maintaining a distinct sense of national identity. As a matter of fact, 'National identity is not an innate quality in human beings, neither is it acquired naturally as one grows up. Like any other identity, national identity has to be learnt. Important instruments in any learning process are various kinds of audiovisual aids, and so also in the school of national identity construction. That is why national symbols – flags, coats of arms, national anthems – play such a crucial role in nation building and nation-maintenance'.[2] Simply put, those national symbols decorating the jerseys of national football teams acquire a wholly different meaning, particularly, when taking into account Eric Hobsbawm's argument that a nation might well be reflected in 'a team of eleven named people'.[3]

The essence of national identity and its apparent connection to the game of football cannot be emphasized enough. England claims little success in international football, if any, since the 1966 World Cup feat is still debated (one ponders, 'did the ball cross the line?'), which in turn raises quite an important question that demands a convincing answer: 'Have international football matches ever been manipulated as a state instrument to project nationalism?' According to the master of (scheming) diplomacy, 'for purposes of international soccer, the UK fields four teams: England, Scotland, Wales and Northern Ireland. A single UK team using the best players from each would be even more formidable'.[4] Perhaps, a UK national football team might have been more successful on the pitch, even winning trophies. Yet, the unmistakable essence of nationalism would dictate that sharing a trophy with another three nations is definitely no more significant than maintaining 'independence'. It is simply for this reason that when Jack Straw, Minister of Internal Affairs, suggested in December 2000 that all four nations merge their football prowess into one single national football team, his ill-perceived remark was rejected. Football serves nationalism well, and in the case of the UK it helps demarcate the borders separating one nation from the other. Celebrating your national football team's victory over another nation is 'testament to the enduring significance of nationalism and the nation-state represented by the national team'. For some, as in Benito Mussolini's Italy, it may also serve to promote hostile expansionist plans over neighbouring countries.[5] All in all, taking into account England's rivalry with the other Home Nations; the bitter football rivalries between Germany and any other Central European nation, not to mention her intense matches with England and the Netherlands; the usually heated games between Balkan nations ever since the disintegration of Yugoslavia; the age-old animosity that usually over shadows football matches between Greece and Turkey; and the sheer fact that Israel only joined UEFA to avoid playing its Arab neighbours, it becomes evident that nationalism can, indeed, generate sentiments that may account for the occasional war-like conditions of the game of football.

Needless to say, it is the football matches between national sides that captivate the continent's imagination when the European Championship is contested every four years, as football competitions of the like hardly ever fail to stimulate nationalistic fervour. National flags unfold, past rivalries come to life, and multi-colour regiments of fans dominate stadiums, as the game of football is transformed from sport to battle. Nations employ militaristic emotions, while maintaining a festive atmosphere of course, since national pride is at stake whenever a match draws to a close. Failing an entire nation may have devastating consequences, particularly, when defeat revives memories of an old foe. Even the integrated Europe cannot escape such emotions, as football seems to pervade all notions of assimilation, and much like culture it helps emphasize collective identity. It is imperative, therefore, to study the symbols representing some of Europe's finest national football associations. For structural purposes, UEFA's coefficients have been adopted, as employed by the European football governing body in the draw for the Euro 2012 finals in Poland and Ukraine.

Spain

Founded in 1909, the Royal Spanish Football Federation (*Real Federación Española de Fútbol*) was best owed royal status by King Alfonso XIII in 1913. The Spanish football governing body joined FIFA in 1913, but was represented in its inaugural meeting by Madrid FC – the same club that is today known as Real Madrid Club de Fútbol. Decorating the jersey of the Spanish national football team is the country's coat of arms, also imposed on the national flag. It comprises six arms representing the Kingdoms of Castile (gold castle against a red background), Granada (pomegranate flower), Leon (red lion in a white background) and Navarre (golden chains); the Crown of Aragon (red and yellow stripes); and the House of Bourbon (fleur-de-lis). Complementing the Spanish arms are the Pillars of Hercules (the ancient name for the Straits of Gibraltar) on either side of the arms; the Imperial Crown of the Holy Roman Empire; and the Spanish Royal crown. Unlike the historico-cultural wealth that characterizes the Spanish coat of arms, the emblem of the Royal Spanish Football Federation has no apparent symbolic significance.

Instead, what is rather interesting is the obscurity usually surrounding the national football team of Spain. The performance of the Spanish national football team notwithstanding, the full-hearted support it rarely receives from the Spaniards is commendable. Catalans and Basques, for example, often fail to identify with the Spanish national team due to their distinct national identity. In fact, 'support for the Spanish national team in Catalonia and the Basque Country during the 1982 World Cup in Spain was low-key,'[6] precisely because of how people in Catalonia and the Basque Country perceived the Spanish national team. Yet, this bizarre phenomenon is no longer exclusive to Catalans and Basques alone merely because it might have started 'with Cataluña and Euskadi playing international friend lies, but now one sees Cantabria, Galicia, Aragón, Andalucía, Castilla y León, etc., having their own national uniforms and kits and playing 'international' matches against long established nation-states such as Bulgaria and Brazil alongside fixtures with other 'new' nations such as Latvia'.[7] As for the national team's mediocre performance of the past at international level, Ball suggested that it 'may under perform due to players coming from separatist regions perhaps causing friction in the dressing-room'.[8] What might have been an intriguing case-study for the social sciences and the humanities is no longer for the recent success of the Spanish national football team has proved such a hypothesis entirely wrong.

The Netherlands

The Netherlands, and Denmark, set-up the first national football association in continental Europe. Founded in 1889, the *Nederlandse Voetbal en Atletiek Bond* was clearly not entirely devoted to the game of football, since it also included athletics. A truly football-oriented association was established six years later when athletics were dropped to give way to the *Nederlandse Voetbal Bond*. The Dutch association is one of FIFA's founding members and was granted royal status (*Koninklijke*) by the queen in 1929 to celebrate the association's fortieth anniversary, thus paving the way for the *KoninklijkeNederlandse Voetbal Bond* (Royal Netherlands Football Association) to regulate Dutch football. Governing Dutch football was, initially, a rather difficult task considering the country's religious segregation. In fact, the Royal Netherlands Football Association only succeeded in becoming the ultimate national football governing body as late as 1940. In the interim period, a distinct football association co-existed, until the two eventually merged. It is important to note that 'the founder members of the Dutch FA were drawn from the cities of North and South Holland, these provinces being the most powerful, economically and politically, and historically the bastions of the Protestant commercial class'.[9] In other words, in the religiously divided society that was the Netherlands at the time, football managed to survive and was even employed as a unifying force.

Playing its football in the famous orange, the *Oranje* have only claimed one trophy, the European Championship of 1988 in Germany, but has been credited with the invention of 'Total Football'. Historically, 'the colour orange is, of course, the symbol of the Dutch royal family, deriving from the town of Orange in Provence, a possession acquired by the (originally German) royal house of Nassau'.[10] Symbolizing creativity, while also representing the Greek god Dionysos, the Dutch coat of arms was adopted by King William Orange-Nassau. As for the orange crowned lion that represents the Royal Netherlands Football Association, it derives from the arms of Nassau, even though a lion denoted to Burgundian Netherlands as well and, later, the national arms of the Dutch republic.

Germany

The German Football Association (*Deutscher Fußball Bund*) was founded in Leipzig in 1900 during a meeting held at the Mariengarten restaurant. For a considerable period of time, the *Deutscher Fußball Bund* represented football in West Germany alone, until the reunification of Germany in 1990. Football in East Germany was regulated by the *Deutscher Fußball Verband der DDR*. As in the Netherlands, Germany is yet another European country that benefited much from football's unique properties. There is no shadow of doubt that the so-called 'Miracle of Berne' (1954) commands our undivided attention for the unexpected success of the national football team strengthened a deep sense of collective identity among the West Germans.

The emblem of the German Football Association, on the other hand, deserves little mention for it merely features its initials in a seemingly stylized manner. It is the national football team's emblem that merits attention, as it displays a rather dominant symbol of power – the imperial eagle. The imperial eagle derives from the coat of arms of Germany, and has served as symbol of both the German Republic and the Weimar Republic, later modified to cater to the needs of Adolph Hitler's Nazi Party.

Despite the symbol's links to Nazi Germany, the imperial eagle retained its cultural significance throughout the Cold War by representing the Federal Republic of Germany and, today, the unified Germany. As concerns Germany's national flag, 'the black-red-gold flag had been the symbol of the nationalist movement since 1848', however, 'Otto von Bismarck preferred a tricolour comprising the Prussian black and white and the Hanseatic red which became the black-white-red banner of the German Empire until 1919. Subsequently, the Weimar Assembly stuck to the name "German Empire" but changed its colours to black-red-gold'.[11]

Italy

Azzuri is the ingenious epithet that follows Italy's national football team everywhere. Deriving from the Italian word for blue, *azzuro*, it makes reference to the well-known blue jerseys worn by the players. Historically, blue was the colour of the House of Savoy, the royal family of Italy; nevertheless, Italy's first attempt at international football witnessed her national team playing in plain white 'largely because, as the Football Commission reports of the time state, white shirts were the cheapest available'.[12]

The national football team of Italy is governed by the Italian Football Federation (*Federazione Italiana del Giuoco del Calcio*), founded in 1898. The governing body of Italian football is certainly one of the most exciting national associations in Europe, devoting much of its energies on trophies and scandals alike. The emblematic figure representing the Italian Football Federation is somewhat identical to the Italian national flag, with the exception of the four five-pointed gold stars displayed alongside. The stars stand for Italy's secular symbol, the so-called *Stellone d'Italia*, which derives from the non-heraldic coat of arms of the Italian Republic. Against the background of a wheel of industry, clearly symbolizing the ethos of an industrious nation, the star is displayed between two branches of olive and oak, representing peace and strength, respectively. The star is also decorating the head of *Italia Turrita*, a personification of Italy in the form of a Mediterranean female figure; nevertheless, a similar star was also depicted on the coat of arms of the House of Savoy. The true origins of *Stellone d'Italia* notwithstanding, there is no definitive interpretation on the number of stars, although it may well relate to what is certainly an amazing collection of four World Cup trophies (1934, 1938, 1982 and 2006).

England

An impressive emblem that dates back to the times of Richard the Lion heart are the three lions representing with much grace the association credited for organizing the game of football. Also known as 'The FA', the English Football Association was founded as early as 1863 and was the first to regulate football competitions and organize international matches. When the English national football team played its first international match against Scotland in 1872, the players' jerseys were clearly dominated by an emblem displaying three lions. History tells us that 'Richard's heraldic red shield incorporated three golden lions to represent the kingdom of England. As such, this shield still appears on the Royal arms today (alongside Scottish and Irish emblems) which, since 1603, have been supported by a crowned lion and a unicorn. Given its origins, history and current use on the monarch's arms, the English lion must be read politically as connotative of royalty in addition to its more overt communication of the qualities of power, bravery and courage. In a sporting context, too, the king of the beasts is often associated with English football. It has long been the emblem of the FA, for instance, and, as such, appears in triplicate on the shirts of the England national team. It is not altogether surprising, then, that the patriotic, royalist symbol of the lion should be so extensively employed as a metaphor by football journalists reporting the England team's exploits'.[13]

Interestingly, when England played hosts to the 1996 European Championship, uplifting the fans spirit around the stadium just as it boosted the players' efforts on the pitch was the 'Three Lions' song, which continually reminded all football aficionados that "football's coming home", clearly underlining the game' origins. Furthermore, 'the representations of English national identity offered by the media in their reporting of English football and, especially, of the England national team are based upon a cluster of perceptions which, we would contend, derive from and feed into wider assumptions in the national imagined community dating from the imperial era that serve to define "Englishness".[14] Along the same lines, the red-cross-on-a-white-background flag of St. George, too, has the all-important qualities for generating a distinct sense of collective identity. In point of fact, 'looking back to the crowd at the 1966 World Cup, barely any St. George crosses can be seen as the stands appear to be waving British Union flags'. As late as Italia '90 the balance between the two flags is half and half. But from 1997, as the devolution plans of the New Labour government took shape and Wales, Scotland and Northern Ireland all acquired a significant level of political autonomy, the Englishness of the football team rose in importance',[15] since the English football supporters 'waved an old flag in a new way. Until 1996, England fans had always used the red-and-white-and-blue Union Jack while the red-on-white flag of St. George was tainted by association with the far right. Now the English – as opposed to the British – took to St. George with relish'.[16] On the whole, there is no doubt that the English national football team manifests national pride.

Russia

The history of the Russian Football Union (*Rossiiski Futbolnyi Soyuz*) dates back to 1912 when a similar short-lived football organization was founded. Succeeded by the All-Union Supreme Council for Physical Culture in 1929, the popular game was properly governed when an exclusive association was founded in 1935 and after the Ministry of Sport had first taken charge of all sporting activities. During the times of the Soviet Union, football was habitually governed by the local authorities, although an independent Football Federation of the USSR had been founded in 1959. When the Soviet Union disintegrated, the Russian Football Union emerged anew. The national football team of the Soviet Union made its debut in 1912 during the Olympic Games in Stockholm 'wearing yellow jerseys with the Romanov emblem – a double-headed eagle – emblazoned on their chests'.[17] Today, it is the exact same double-headed eagle that dominates the national coat of arms of the Russian Federation, as well as the logo of the Russian Football Union (on top of a ball in Russia's white-blue-and-red colours).

The eagle derives from the arms of the Russian Empire, however, its origins date back to the times of the Byzantine Empire. Ivan III, Grand Duke of Moscow, adopted the symbol of the Byzantine Empire in 1497 after he wedded Sofia Paleologou, niece of the Byzantine Emperor Constantine; nevertheless, the double-headed eagle first featured in its present form under the Romanov Dynasty. It was during the times of the Romanovs that the three crowns, the sceptre and the orb were added. The shield protecting the eagle's breast depicts St. George slaying a dragon. The figure of St. George in this posture is a national symbol of Russia, also featured on the capital's coat of arms for he is the patron-saint of Moscow. Interestingly, while 'Russia remained a state without unifying, generally recognized national symbols', when Boris Yeltsin was in office, it was apparently football that initiated Russia's quest for appropriate national symbols when Football Club Spartak Moscow 'complained to Putin that the Glinka song [used as national anthem] was impossible to sing and claimed that this situation had led to 'a loss of morale and dip in form'.[18]

Croatia

The story behind the foundation of the Croatian Football Federation (*Hrvatski Nogometni Savez*) is a mirror image of the country's turbulent past. Founded in 1912 in Zagreb, the activities of the Croatian Football Federation were suspended when the First World War broke out. Upon the formation of the Kingdom of Yugoslavia, the Croatian Football Federation was then absorbed by the Yugoslav Football Association (*Nogometni Savez Jugoslavije*), which had been set up in 1919, also based in Zagreb. When the latter was suitably moved to Belgrade, the Croatian Football Federation refused to relocate and was restructured in 1939 in what proved to be a farsighted decision for the disintegration of the Kingdom of Yugoslavia after the end of the Second World War paved the way for its independence from its Yugoslav patron. Of course the Kingdom of Yugoslavia was succeeded by the Socialist Federal Republic of Yugoslavia, yet the Croatian Football Federation maintained its integrity and enjoyed relative autonomy up until the collapse of the Yugoslav Federation.

Once Croatia gained independence, the authority of the Croatian Football Federation was fully restored as well. Evidently, the Croatian national football team almost immediately became 'a powerful symbol of the new Croatia and was exploited as such by the national president, Franjo Tudjman'.[19] Reflecting the mass appeal of the national football team, the emblem of the Croatian Football Federation resembles much the national coat of arms. It depicts a shield that displays the red-and-white *šahovnica* intersected by a vertical bar that features the federation's initials with a ball underneath. The famous checkerboard, the same one that once served the causes of the Ustaše, was first adopted by Croatian kings around the tenth century before it was recognized as the official national symbol of Croatia in the nineteenth century.

Greece

The emblem of the Hellenic Football Federation (*Ελληνική Ποδοσφαιρική Ομοσπονδία*), founded in 1926, is as unimaginative as to feature a ball in the blue-and-white national colours with a map of Greece at its centre. The emblem displayed on the shirts of the national football team that rendered the world of football speechless when it claimed the 2004 European Championship that was hosted in Portugal, however, features the national flag of Greece, as derived from the national coat of arms. Making up the flag of Greece is a white cross representing all things Christian, Eastern Orthodox Christianity more precisely, and nine blue-and-white horizontal lines that succinctly describe the country's war-scarred history. It has been so designed to express the national axiom of Greece, 'freedom or death' (*Ελευθερίαή Θάνατος*), considering its nine syllabuses (*E-λευ-θε-ρί-αή Θά-να-τος*), and was first employed as a war-cry during the Greek War of Independence against the Ottomans.

Portugal

The Portuguese Football Federation (*Federação Portuguesa de Futebol*) was founded in 1914 following the merging of three regional football associations. Representing the Portuguese Football Federation is the cross of the Order of Christ of Portugal, along with the five shields featured on the national coat of arms. The Order of Christ of Portugal was in fact a military order that has its origins in the ranks of the Knights Templar and was set up in an attempt to defend the Iberian Peninsula against the invading Saracens. It was in fact formed at the request of King Diniz in order to strengthen the first line of defence, which had been weakened following the vacuum created by the eventual ecclesiastical suppression of the Knights Templar. Sanctioned by both Pope John XXII and the King of Portugal, the Order of Christ assumed significant powers much like their predecessors in an attempt to defend Christianity. The five shields, suitably placed to form a cross, were conceived after a vision King Afonso I had before the Battle of Ourique. Historically, the five shields represent the emirates ruled by the defeated Moorish kings, namely, Badajoz, Beja, Elvas, Évora and Seville. The white marks featured on each shield, allegedly, symbolize the five wounds of Jesus. Nevertheless, their number was never set since Afonso Henriques' rule came to an end, nor is there any historical evidence available to support this interpretation.

Sweden

The Swedish Football Association (*Svenska Fotbollförbundet*) was founded in 1904. Its emblem derives from the national flag of Sweden and displays the yellow Scandinavian cross against a blue background, the colours originating from the royal coat of arms dating back to the thirteenth century. According to Swedish mythology, while away on a military expedition against their Finnish neighbours, King Eric saw a gold cross in the (blue) sky and later adopted a similar coat of arms. History, on the other hand, dictates that King Charles Knutsson was the first to adopt a banner that resembled the modern-day flag of Sweden, as well as a similar coat of arms, inspired by the banners of King Magnus Birgersson (1275) and King Albert of Mecklenburg (1364).

Czech Republic

The Football Association of the Czech Republic (*Českomoravský Fotbalový Svaz*) was founded in 1901, but was suspended by the Football Association of Czechoslovakia (*Československý Fotbalový Svaz*) for a period of seventy years (1922–1993). It emerged again, as an independent body, soon after the partition of Czechoslovakia and the subsequent independence of the Czech Republic. The emblem of the Czech Football Association depicts a ball and the national coat of arms, which represents the historical regions that make up the modern-day republic, namely, Bohemia,

Moravia, and Silesia. The coat of arms of Bohemia features a lion with two tails against a red background; the coat of arms of Moravia displays a red-and-white chequered eagle against a blue background; and Silesia's coat of arms illustrates a black eagle with a crescent across its breast against a yellow background. Interestingly, two sections of the national coat of arms feature a lion: one lion stands for Bohemia, whereas the second represents the entire nation.

It is noteworthy that football's all-important qualities were once again highlighted in the case of Czechoslovakia. The draw for the 1994 FIFA World Cup qualifying rounds took place on 8 December 1991, with Czechoslovakia being one of the thirty-nine European contestants. However, Czechoslovakia dissolved on 1 January 1993, several months before the national football team's international obligations were completed. Justifiably so, the national football team of Czechoslovakia only played three matches. For the remaining seven football games, a team named the Representatives of Czechs and Slovaks replaced the national football team that was left without a nation to serve. It is under such conditions that the game of football has the capacity to demonstrate that no matter the starting line-up of the team, any football players could well represent people that were neighbours not so long ago.

Denmark

As already mentioned above, the Danish Football Association (*Dansk Boldspil-Union*) is one of the two continental football associations that came to life first, founded in 1889. Even though the game of football is, supposedly, male dominated, football at national level in Denmark is represented by an emblem that is symbolically associated with femininity.As it happens, both the Danish national football team and the football association are represented by a flower. While the Red Clover is considered as the national flower of Denmark, nevertheless, it is a Marguerite Daisy (*Argyranthemum Frutescens*) that seems to decorate their emblem.

France

The French Football Federation (*Fédération Française de Football*), founded in 1919, came to replace the many different sports organizations that regulated football at regional level, thus replacing the*Comité Français Interfédéral* and its predecessor, the *Union des Sociétés Françaises de Sports Athlétiques*. It is important to note that 'till the First World War, no less than five different organizations claimed the right to be the French national FA and this was not unified until 1918',[20]clearly reflecting the degree of social, religious, political and, above all, territorial division of the French society of the time.

Representing the French Football Federation is the 'national bird of France, the Gallic cockerel, which duly appears, crowning with some pride of late, on top of the letters FFF on the shirts of the national team'.[21] The *Coq Gaulois*serves as a national symbol of France since the Middle Ages. During the Renaissance, the Gallic cock represented the emerging French nation, but gained immense symbolic significance as a symbol of the Revolution. When the French Republic gave way to Napoleon's Empire, the Gallic cock was replaced by the more dominant eagle, until the former was restored. Nowadays, the *Coq Gaulois* represents France in all international sports competitions.

Republic of Ireland

Formerly known as the Football Association of the Irish Free State, the Football Association of Ireland was founded in 1921, in the face of opposition from England, Scotland, Wales and Northern Ireland. Much unlike the intriguing history of the Football Association of Ireland, its emblem is unimpressive for it simply displays a futuristic-like ball in the green of Ireland.

Ukraine

Following the independence of Ukraine, the Ukrainian Football Federation (*Федерація Футболу України*) was founded in 1991. The emblem of both the Ukrainian Football Federation and its national team, a trident, derives from the coat of arms of Ukraine. Historically, the trident was a cultural symbol of the Slavs that resided in what is modern-day Ukraine and was also featured on the seal and banners of the Rurik Dynasty. Different interpretations suggest that the trident may symbolize the Holy Trinity, a preying falcon, or an arched bow with an arrow. Another interpretation that delves into religion indicates that the trident, in its present figure, may represent an anchor – an extremely significant religious symbol in pre-Christian times. Today, a stylized yellow trident against a blue background makes up the national coat of arms of Ukraine.

Poland

The Polish Football Federation (*Polski Związek Piłki Nożnej*) was founded in 1919, exactly a year after Poland's independence. The emblem of the Polish Football Federation displays the same eagle featured on the national coat of arms superimposed on the red-and-white national flag. According to a legend, Lech (the founder of Poland, also known as *Lechia*), Czech (founder of Bohemia), and Rus (founder of Ruthenia, modern-day Belarus, Russia and Ukraine), all brothers, were once on a hunting expedition when they got separated. Lech, the story goes, came across a beautiful place where a white eagle was guarding its nest. He set up his camp there, named the area Griezno (from *gniazdo*, meaning 'nest' in Polish) and adopted the white eagle as his emblem. Historically, a similar eagle decorated the coat of arms of the Piast Dynasty, before King Premyslas II decided to adopt the eagle as part of the Polish national coat of arms. As for the national colours of Poland (red and white), they derive from the coat of arms of Poland and Lithuania, as the Polish Eagle and Lithuanian Pursuer both appear in white against a red background.

Conclusion

From the sixteen nations that contested the 2012 UEFA European Championship in Poland and Ukraine, twelve football teams' emblem sport their national coat of arms, one nation's emblem displays its national flag, another two employ national symbols, and one nation simply makes use of a stylized ball for a badge. Having categorized these nations on a regional basis, as per the United Nations Statistics Division,[22] some rather interesting findings emerge almost mechanically.

What the national football associations and the respective national football teams from Southern Europe (Croatia, Greece, Italy, Portugal and Spain) and Eastern Europe (the Czech Republic, Poland, Russia and Ukraine) have in common is the fact that they all feature their national coat of arms for an emblem, thus the reason these two European regions are assessed as one. With the notable exception of the Ukrainian Football Federation (est.1991), the remaining south and east European nations founded their football associations between 1898 and 1926 – an admittedly crucial period of time for the rise of nationalism in Europe. A coat of arms, more often than not comprising the rather dominant icon of a shield, is a heraldic symbol and was first employed several centuries ago so as to better signify royal families and relevant forms of authority. The term heraldry derives from the Anglo-Saxon *here* (army) and *wald* (strength), although it may also have its origins in the Old French for 'herald' (*herault*), or else 'the messenger or proclaimer who in medieval times often exercised the function of a diplomat. Merely by their appearance, their costumes bore witness to their membership of a group or sovereign power, so that they would be unmistakably recognized from the enemy camp'.[23] Through the lens of heraldry, nobility acquired a distinct form for illustrating history and culture almost effortlessly when communities, then cities and then states made use of coats of arms to express their identity. Needless to say, to the ethnic nations of southern and eastern Europe the symbolic properties of a coat of arms would have rendered any other emblem ineffectual, given its accuracy in representing a nation well whether playing at home or away. The sense of collective identity emanating from such powerful symbols must have appealed to those newly established football associations, and probably to the independent Ukraine several decades later.

The civic nations of Western Europe (Germany, France and the Netherlands) and Northern Europe (Denmark, England, the Republic of Ireland and Sweden), on the other hand, seem more diverse in their selection of a suitable emblem to represent the nation in the world of football. While the year of foundation of all seven national football associations coincides (1889–1921) with that of their southern and eastern European counterparts, it is intriguing that only three feature a coat of arms for an emblem. Of course the coat of arms would hold an eminent position, however, in the long-lived monarchies of the Netherlands and England it is the royal family's arms that have been employed, whereas in the case of Germany it is the national coat of arms that decorates the football players' jerseys. As already noted above, the emblem of the Swedish Football Association while based on the national flag of Sweden, it is, of course, inspired by the national coat of arms. Only the football associations of France, Denmark and the Republic of Ireland have opted for an emblem different from the national coat of arms. The French Football Federation has adopted the Gallic cock, as have all other national sports organizations in France that participate in international competitions. The Danish Football Association, too, has opted for what appears to be the national flower, but not exactly. As for the emblem representing the Republic of Ireland national football association, stylized or not, it is nothing more than a ball. Perhaps the prominent national symbol of Ireland that is the shamrock would have served the same cause far better.

With the notable exception of the Football Association of Ireland, the emblems of the remaining fifteen national football associations that were represented in the stadiums of Poland and Ukraine clearly document an important aspect of their culture and history. Hardly surprising, I hear you say. Indeed, of the fifty-three members that altogether make up the Union of European Football Associations (UEFA), a staggering forty-three national football associations have employed their national coat of arms, flags or other similar national symbols. The ethnocentric approach adopted by the vast majority of UEFA's members makes one thing certain; the very same banners that once headed the advance of European armies today lead national football teams.

Notes

1. European Commission, *Studies on Education and Sport*, 78.
2. Kolstø, 'National Symbols as Signs of Unity and Division', 676.
3. Hobsbawm, *Nations and Nationalism since 1780*, 43.
4. Kissinger, 'World Cup According to Character', 246.
5. Kuper, *Football Against the Enemy*, 25.
6. Duke and Crolley, *Football, Nationality, and the State*, 41.
7. Wharton, 'Reflections on the New fiesta nacional(ista),' 605.
8. Ball, *Morbo*, 218.
9. Wagg, 'On the Continent,' 105.
10. Winner, 'The Orange Party', 157.
11. Merkel, 'The Hidden Social and Political History', 78.
12. Agnew, *Forza Italia*, 55.
13. Crolley and Hand, *Football, Europe and the Press*, 28.
14. Crolley and Hand, *Football, Europe and the Press*, 31.
15. Goldblatt, *The Ball is Round*, 736.
16. Winner, *Those Feet*, 86.
17. Goldblatt, *The Ball is Round*, 168.
18. Kolstø, 'National symbols as signs of unity and division', 686.
19. Wilson, *Behind the Curtain*, 146.
20. Crolley and MacWilliam, *Fields of Glory, Paths of Gold*, 23.
21. Crolley and Hand, *Football, Europe and the Press*, 63.
22. Composition of macro-geographical (continental) regions, geographical sub-regions, and selected economic and other groupings
23. Frutiger, *Signs and Symbols*, 318.

References

Agnew, Paddy. *Forza Italia: A Journey in Search of Italy and its Football*. London: Ebury Press, 2006.
Ball, Phil. *Morbo: The Story of Spanish Football*. London: WSC Books, 2003.
Crolley, Liz, and David Hand. *Football, Europe and the Press*. London and Portland: Frank Cass Publishers, 2002.
Crolley, Kevin, and Rob MacWilliam. *Fields of Glory, Paths of Gold: The History of European Football*. Edinburgh and London: Mainstream Publishing.
Duke, Vic, and Liz Crolley. *Football, Nationality, and the State*. New York: Addison Wesley Longman, 1996.
European Commission, DG Education & Culture. *Studies on Education and Sport, Sport and Multiculturalism*. Final Report by PMP in partnership with the Institute of Sport and Leisure Policy. Loughborough University, August 2004, 78.
Frutiger, Adrian. *Signs and Symbols: Their Design and Meaning*. Trans. Andrew Bluhm. Hereford: Studio Editions, 1989.
Goldblatt, David. *The Ball is Round: A Global History of Football*. London: Viking, an imprint of Penguin Books, 2006.
Hobsbawm, Eric. *Nations and Nationalism since 1780: Programme, Myth, Reality*. Cambridge: Cambridge University Press, 1990.

King, Anthony. *The European Ritual: Football in the New Europe*. Aldershot: Ashgate, 2003.

Kissinger, Henry. 'World Cup According to Character', *The Los Angeles Times*, June 29, 1986.

Kolstø, Pål. 'National Symbols as Signs of Unity and Division'. *Ethnic and Racial Studies 29*, no. 4 (2006): 676–701.

Kuper, Simon. *Football Against the Enemy*. London: Orion, 2003.

Merkel, Udo. 'The Hidden Social and Political History of the German Football Association (DFB) 1900-50', *Soccer & Society 1*, no. 2 (2000): 167–186.

United Nations. 'Composition of macro geographical (continental) regions, geographical sub-regions, and selected economic and other groupings'. http://unstats.un.org/unsd/methods/m49/m49regin.htm#europe

Wagg, Stephen. 'On the Continent: Football in the Societies of North West Europe'. In *Giving the Game Away: Football, Politics and Culture on Five Continents*, ed. Stephen Wagg, 103–124. London and New York: Leicester University Press, 1995.

Wharton, Barrie. 'Reflections on the New fiesta nacional (ista): Soccer and Society in Modern Spain'. *Soccer & Society 8*, no. 4 (2007): 601–613.

Wilson, Jonathan. *Behind the Curtain: Travels in Eastern European Football*. London: Orion Books, 2006.

Winner, David. *Those Feet: An Intimate History of English Football*, London: Bloomsbury, 2006.

Winner, David. 'The Orange Party'. In *Hooligan Wars: Causes and Effects of Football Violence*, ed. Mark Perryman, 155–164. Edinburgh and London: Mainstream, 2001.

Playing with tension: national charisma and disgrace at Euro 2012

Alex Law

Division of Sociology, University of Abertay, Dundee, UK

By the time of Euro 2012, deepening tensions of nationalism and internal social struggles were developing across Europe in worsening conditions of systemic crisis. The official football ideology of UEFA conceives Euro 2012 as a civilizing platform for mutual respect and brotherhood between competing nations. In contrast, what I call Hyper-Critical Theory conceives of football competitions like Euro 2012 as part of a de-civilising 'sports mode of production' that necessarily produces crisis conditions, alienation and violence on a mass scale, fostering nationalism, militarism and racism. Between these polar perspectives, the figurational sociology of sport associated with Norbert Elias proposes that major international football competitions like Euro 2012 creates and dissipates contingent tensions of 'group charisma' and 'group disgrace'. Study of Euronews 'post-national' coverage of Euro 2012 allows their explanatory adequacy to be compared. In a competition structure like the Euros no social group – players, officials, media or fans – is able to disregard entirely the field capabilities of the 'best minority of 11' in the serious game of exemplifying the group charisma of nations.

Introduction

Suitably ambiguous, the official slogan for Euro 2012 was 'Creating History Together'. For UEFA (Union des Associations Européennes de Football), this reflected the fact that the tournament was being held for the first time in post-Soviet central and eastern Europe, Poland and Ukraine. The 'history' referred to is understood to be simultaneously *football* history and *European* history.[1] Self-consciously 'historical' the competition slogan expressed something of the tension between the dual civilising missions of football and the European state formation process. Since the 1940s, core European nations were released from a revenge cycle of violence founded on the national humiliation and collective shame of total war, mass atrocities, occupation, defeat and declining state power.[2] Yet, with a weak European public sphere and with no Europe-wide state form to concentrate and centralize the means of violence, Europe remains dangerously fractured between rival states.

Euro 2012 took place amidst collective fears and insecurities brought on by economic and political crises. Historically, conditions of institutional crisis generate and heighten political, ethnic and nationalist conflicts and anxieties. The crisis in Europe operates through an ideological prism of irresponsible states and nationalist stereotypes.[3] States covered by the derogatory acronym 'PIGS' (Portugal, Ireland, Greece, Spain) are charged as incompetent and parasitic, supporting a supposedly indulgent national culture with surplus revenue generated by core European institutions. Far from the ideal of continental unity enshrined in the sports ideology of the European Championship, the European state system was rent with internal crisis.

In some ways, football functions as an intermediary conscience collective in the absence of a European public sphere.[4] Formed in 1954 with 25 members, the number of national football associations belonging to UEFA grew rapidly in post-Soviet Europe to 53 by Euro 2012. Typically, national football associations are more or less congruent with the nation/state, with the four national football associations of the UK – England, Scotland, Wales and northern Ireland – something of an exceptional case. Competitive football and competitive nationalism are tethered together. While there may be some evidence of a shallow European identity at previous European Championships, this remains subordinate to the reproduction of nationalist perceptual frames.[5] The football field is never an autonomous zone, set free from other fields of power. International football is always a field of tensions. For instance, around the same time that 'little' Denmark rejected, at least initially, the Maastricht Treaty as reflecting over-weaning German power, the Danish defeat of Germany in the Euro 1992 final stimulated a spasm of anti-German nationalism.[6] Similarly, the violent reaction of Zinedine Zidane in the 2006 World Cup final is inexplicable without an understanding of 'games within games', where race, gender and nationality intersect as antagonistic social fields on the football field.[7]

Analysis of Euronews coverage of Euro 2012 reveals something of the tensions between competitive football and competitive nationalism in conditions of the European state system in crisis. Broadcasting simultaneously in eleven languages,[8] Euronews is one of the few venues for a European public sphere.[9] Its founding ideology aims to produce 'European news for Europeans'.[10] As the semi-official news media of Europeanism, Euronews presents certain advantages for gauging the extent to which tensions between nations and states within Europe are channelled by 'the other Euro' of international football. For one thing, Euronews covered Euro 2012 from a transnational perspective rather than the banal nationalism that routinely frames news and sports media.[11] For this study, a corpus was assembled of all Euronews broadcasts in English that mentioned Euro 2012 in any context – sporting, economic, political, cultural – in the weeks before, during and after the tournament from May to July 2012. Under the deal struck between UEFA and the European Broadcasting Union (EBU), Euronews did not have broadcasting rights for the tournament.[12] Instead, Euronews bulletins relied on analysis of still photography and computer graphics of play. This produced a more detached and analytical effect than live action replays of dramatic moments. As much emphasis was given to events outside the stadium as coverage of on-field play, giving prominence to the interactions between fans of different nationalities.

If Euronews coverage falls somewhat short of forming a European public sphere founded on factual impartiality, it nonetheless expresses some of the emergent tensions and dynamics between opposing national groups in a supposedly de-politicized international sports context. While Euronews cannot be considered a neutral arbiter between states, it shares with UEFA an ideological commitment to the civilizing function of globalized Europeanism. It also provides empirical representations for examining the sociology of emotional, political and economic tensions generated by international football. At the polar extreme of official UEFA football ideology, what I will call 'Hyper-Critical Theory' denies that football can perform any civilising function; if anything football deepens the de-civilizing violence of contemporary capitalism. Between official sports ideology and Hyper-Critical Theory, the figurational sociology of sport pioneered by Norbert Elias and Eric Dunning more dialectically identifies international football as a serious but contained game that generates and alleviates heightened emotional and bodily tensions in exciting but generally peaceful ways.

Three perspectives on football

For official sports ideology football creates a civilizing space for national groups to make contact with and to recognize each other below the level of formal political structures. Since the 1984 European Championship in France, fans of national teams attend the Euros in increased numbers, resulting in generally peaceful contact with each other, although fan hooliganism remained a constant concern for authorities.[13] As fan mobility increased and transnational media audiences for the competition grew, UEFA aligned itself explicitly with the European Union ideal of 'unity in diversity'. UEFA identifies with the civilising effects of the European state system that pulled Europe out of wartime devastation and national hatreds into continental prosperity and peace.

UEFA's Fair Play code attempts to moderate the conduct of players, officials and fans under an ideology of 'the sporting spirit'. As UEFA state: 'The objective of activities in favour of fair play is to foster a sporting spirit, as well as the sporting behaviour of players, team officials and spectators, thereby increasing the enjoyment of all those involved in the game'.[14] Officials are required to actively moderate any excesses of fans and players: 'Positive and negative aspects of the behaviour of team officials should be assessed; e.g. whether they calm or provoke angry players or fans, how they accept the referee's decisions, etc'.[15] For their part, players should control their emotions, even when decisions are unfairly given against them: 'A positive attitude towards the referees should be rewarded by high marks, including the acceptance of doubtful decisions without protest'.[16] Although very few fans will have ever read official regulations, they are expected by UEFA to create an exciting atmosphere but were also instructed to 'respect' certain boundaries of behaviour and avoid gratuitously offensive, threatening or violent behaviour towards opposing fans, players or officials.

> The crowd is considered to be a natural component of a football game. The support of the fans may contribute to the success of their team. The crowd is *not expected to* watch the game in silence. Encouragement of teams by shouting, singing, etc. may have a positive influence on the atmosphere, in accordance with the spirit of fair play. The spectators are, however, *expected to* respect the opposing team and the referee. They *should appreciate* the performance of the opposition, even if they emerge as the winners. *They must in no way* intimidate or frighten the opposing team, the referee or opposing supporters.[17]

UEFA freights civilized sporting conduct through the injunction to observe an affirmative football ideology that at all times respects authority. In so doing, official football ideology consolidates the nationalist self-perception of fans, national associations and media alike.

In stark contrast to official sports ideology, for Hyper-Critical Theory competitions like Euro 2012 only serve to exacerbate violent rivalries between nations. Hyper-Critical Theory derives principally from 'the Frankfurt School' of

Max Horkheimer, Theodor Adorno, Herbert Marcuse and Jurgen Habermas among others, alongside related theorists like Siegfried Kracauer and Walter Benjamin.[18] In the exercise of disciplined obedience to rules sport infantilizes and enslaves adult males in purposeless displays of pseudo-military aggression, producing the stupefying effect of what Adorno called 'meaningless activity with a specious seriousness and significance'.[19] From these premises, a more polemical Hyper-Critical Theory of sport emerged, represented by Jean-Marie Brohm, Bero Rigauer, Gerhard Vinnai and Marc Perelman. For Hyper-Critical Theory, forced bodily repetition in professional football reveals a brutalizing form of mass suffering raised to the level of a global spectacle, a self-mutilating training and compensation for the loss of free and spontaneous play. Football staves off boredom and monotony only by reintroducing it in a more compulsive, violent form. Like capitalist work relations, it dulls free play, moral worth and rational thought.[20] Spectators at Euro 2012 were reduced to a geometrically undifferentiated stadium mass, emotionally regulated by the psycho-acoustics of the crowd's voice, the playing of national anthems, team presentations, flag waving, as well as the wider ideological function of media communications in news and sports programming. Subject to a field of heightened sound and vision critical thought seems impossible and violence routine: 'The violence of seeing is constantly activated by the violence of successive shocks arousing extraordinary emotions; seeing means literally accepting violence and internalizing it as one's vector of inclination; seeing means being in permanent shock without being aware of it'.[21]

Given football's predisposition towards violence identified by Hyper-Critical Theory, Euro 2012 appeared perfectly poised to generate large-scale brutality and sadism. Through its fusion with mass media, football relentlessly promotes national chauvinism, racism and xenophobia. As the 'sport mode of production' saturates everyday life competitive nationalism and competitive football increasingly define each other. Perelman advances a categorical critique of the true 'essence' of sport as endemic violence. In a society bereft of collective projects, 'sport flattens everything as it passes and *becomes the sole project of a society without projects*'.[22] Humiliated by the lash of globalization, international football allows for the compensatory release of nationalist aggression:

> Sporting nationalism contributes to the *unrestrained behaviour* of overheated supporters and shares in the *generalized violence* of which sport is the most visible public manifestation. *Everywhere* can be found the worship of strength, contempt for weakness, chauvinism, racism, xenophobia, anti-Semitism, homophobia, verbal and physical violence inside and outside stadiums, brutality on *every* ground.[23]

Old ideals about fair play, sportsmanship and self-realization give way to demands for competitive victory at all costs. Team discipline and one-sided specialization recalls military discipline, unthinking and unfeeling obedience and neurotic self-abnegation for the national cause. Professional footballers are 'happy in their suffering and suffer for their happiness'.[24] Collective narcissism and violent domination fantasies are given free-rein: 'All the values of the capitalist jungle are played out in sport: virility, sexual athleticism, physical dominance, the superman, muscle worship, fascistic male chauvinism, racism, sexism, etc.'[25] Large screen technology conjures up a repetitive series of fetish images of athletic reality that transforms the body into a competitive and reified fantasy object, a collective hallucination of the national ideal.

Hyper-Critical Theory has in turn been subject to searching criticism by sports scholars, including hegemony theorists of sport like John Hargeaves and Richard Gruneau, for reducing the more open-ended cultural practices of sport to reified structures of economic domination.[26] For critics, it is an idealist error to erect a totalizing 'sports mode of production' dominating entire nations and continents. Hyper-Critical Theory is contrasted to Adorno's more sophisticated negative dialectic of sport, which retained a utopian aspect in sport's playful promise of a future liberated from instrumental domination.[27] Others suggest that Adorno was engaged merely in ironic exaggeration as a warning about sport's negative side, whereas Hyper-Critical Theory one sidedly elevates the bad side of sport as a fully adequate description of empirical reality.[28] If, as Norbert Elias argued, Adorno clung pessimistically to the belated intellectual authority of Marx, then Hyper-Critical Theory hypostatize *reductio ad absurdum* the inherited authority of theoretical categories from earlier theories, principally Adorno and Marcuse, in place of dynamic social theory adequate to the historical present.[29]

Between the universal critique of sport as unrestrained nationalist violence and UEFA's affirmative promotion of Euro 2012 as a brotherhood of nations, figurational sociology contends that football creates and dissipates tensions between reality and fantasy, play and seriousness, restraint and violence in we-images of international figurations.[30] Rather than a reified object of domination, football engenders historically-specific relations of tension between competing and cooperating groups. To succeed, the internationalisation of football historically required organisational forms at increasing spatial scales of inter-dependency: local, national and transnational. As Norbert Elias classically demonstrated, global sportization was only possible because the state had previously pacified internal space and institutionalised a series of national figurations.[31]

Major international football competitions like Euro 2012 provide a collective focus for negotiating historical tensions of what Elias called 'group charisma' and 'group disgrace'.[32] National group charisma depends on routine forms of interdependence and negotiation of boundaries – ethno-cultural, territorial or political – that distinguish 'we' the insiders sharing something in common from 'them' the outsiders who are different in some respect. Dominant nations attribute to themselves all the characteristics of superior virtue and social grace through self-praise and an exemplary image of the 'minority of the best' and impose on dominated nations feelings of 'group disgrace', inferiority and stigma based on 'they-images' of 'the minority of the worst'. At the level of the nation, images of the best in group charisma and the worst in group disgrace also rely on an exemplary 'minority of 11': the national football team. Group charisma is not a once and for all condition. Nations do not stand in a static polarity to each other but actively form relationships of prestige relative to every other nation.

Unlike the categorical declarations of Hyper-Critical Theory, Elias and Dunning revisited the ancient concepts of 'mimesis' and 'catharsis' to more precisely specify the emotional tensions stimulated by football.[33] For Aristotle, artistic productions like tragic theatre should not to be confused with actual human events. Reality is transposed into a different context. In a mimetic context, extreme emotions may be safely expressed or vicariously enjoyed in contrast to the more serious business of daily routines. A cathartic effect is produced in competitive football, stimulating and resolving emotional tensions in a pleasurable rather than a destructive way.

Mimetic violence transposes real fears and desires into a protected zone of life. It provides an antidote to dull routine. Against a background of unexciting habits and everyday forms of compulsion football opens up a space for expressing heightened tensions within relatively safe confines, compensatory excitement for 'the routinization of affect', a release of strong emotions through the socially permitted stimulation of competitive tensions within certain boundaries:

> One can experience hatred and the desire to kill, defeating opponents and humiliating enemies. One can share making love to the most desirable men and women, experience the anxieties of threatened defeat and the open triumph of victory.[34]

What is forbidden is permitted, albeit selectively and under regulatory pressures of social approval. Feelings of national glory are enjoyed and national reversals endured with equanimity, permitting national 'self-love without bad conscience'.[35]

Elias and Dunning situate the cathartic effect of national triumph over vanquished enemies within the shelter of football's fair trial of organized strength. Elias distinguishes between 'achievement sport' of international competitions and more open-ended 'leisure sport'. In the latter case, playful mimesis exerts autonomy from 'real life' tensions; in the former case, achievement threatens to overwhelm playful tensions: 'In the form of achievement sport, the playful mimetic tensions of leisure sport becomes dominated and patterned by global tensions and rivalries between different states'.[36]

For the cathartic effect to function, mimetic play creates emotional tensions that fluctuate between opposed waves of anxiety and elation, risk and security. Too little or too much in either direction endangers the effect. Too much control over emotional alternation at the boredom pole and football becomes just another monotonous rule-based regime. Too little control and heightened feelings at the excitement pole may break out into real hostilities of physical violence. Football constantly calibrates between the Scylla of disorder and the Charybdis of boredom. Hence, the tone of the game depends on interdependent polarities on the field between teams, attack and defence, within teams, the individual and the team, the referee and the players, and between the field and external controls like spectators, media and traditions of rivalry between teams, fans and nations. As Euronews reported, tensions contingent on the relatively autonomous figuration formed by opposing football teams in competitions like the European Championship will be lost and games made 'meaningless' if results are fixed routinely by criminal organizations attracted by the large fortunes (31/05/12).

Hyper-Critical Theory rejects figurational sociology's accent on the 'controlled decontrolling' of nationalist emotions: 'in the narrow context of the nation, globalized sporting competition no longer helps to contain violence or channel it – as academics such as Norbert Elias and Eric Dunning believe – but rather generates and maintains it, spreading it everywhere'.[37] In places, Brohm asserts that sport serves a cathartic function for capitalism:

> As the biggest mass spectacle, sport operates as a kind of catharsis machine, an apparatus for transforming aggressive drives. Instead of expressing themselves in the class struggle, these drives are absorbed, diverted and neutralized in the sporting spectacle. Sport regulates and socialises aggression by providing permitted models of violence.[38]

By foregrounding state formation processes figurational sociology, unlike hyper-critical theory, tends to relegate the commodification of the sports industry.[39] This lacuna has been addressed more recently by Eric Dunning, who claims that 'most figurational sociologists would also accept much of what Brohm and Rigauer have to say about the penetration of sport by capital, the concomitant processes of commodification and the permeation of sport by work-like structures'.[40] For others figurational sociology simply defies the demands of scientific falsification. Elastic reasoning about the 'controlled decontrolling' of emotions allows for almost every conceivable outcome in sport, ranging from mass violence (de-civilizing breakdown) to self-restraint (civilizing controls).[41] Dunning retorts that such criticism is singularly misplaced. Figurational sociology proposes 'working hypotheses' that remain permanently open to empirical tests of unplanned but patterned historical processes necessary for further theoretical elaboration.[42]

Post-soviet tensions at the Euros

The authorized UEFA narrative of 'Creating History Together' attempted to counter the 'tarnished reputation' of post-Soviet authoritarianism and social decay in the eyes of a global audience, especially the European core. Particularly, damaging to the we-image of Euro hosts Ukraine and Poland was the charge made repeatedly in European core nations of widespread racism in the European periphery. Post-Soviet nations are allegedly prone to the kinds of violent racism that, it is claimed, was removed decades ago from football stadiums in western Europe. Almost, immediately, it was reported that black players training with the Netherlands squad were subjected to racist abuse in Krakow (08/06/12). Of the nations fined by UEFA for racist fans, two were from the European periphery (Croatia and Russia), while the other, Spain, stands at the pinnacle of world football.

Most attention focussed on post-Soviet fan violence. After their first game, UEFA begun disciplinary proceedings against the Football Union of Russia following fan violence, offensive banners and allegations of racist abuse directed at black Czech defender Theodor Gebre Selassie (10/06/12). Violence was reported at Russia's next game with Poland in Warsaw, leading to around 180 arrests. Euronews put this in the context of the history of state formation: 'Tensions run high when both countries meet at sporting events, given the intense rivalry between the two nations that stretches back centuries. Russia occupied Poland for more than 130 years' (12/06/12). Nationalist tensions were further raised by playing the game on a Russian national holiday. On Euronews the following day the Polish Interior Minister Jacek Cichocki emphasized that foreign fans would be given 'special treatment':

> The police investigation is underway and we are fast tracking procedures, *especially in the case of foreigners*. Within the next two days, by Friday the latest, the football violence thugs, *especially Russians*, will be sentenced. Those sentenced will be extradited from Poland. (13/06/12, emphasis added)

However, the report also registered the defensive we-images of offended nationalism, with Russia's football authorities blaming fan violence on provocation by Polish fans.

Back in the core, a heightened fear of post-Soviet violence and racism circulated in the UK media. A former English football hooligan interviewed for Sky Sports

News Special Report, *Ukraine's Hooligans* (25/05/12) warned that English fans, now pacified, are burdened with a decades-old reputation for causing mayhem that could see 'the hunter become the hunted' by violent Ukrainian fans. A few days later, a BBC current affairs programme Panorama's *Euro 2012: Stadiums of Hate* (28/05/12) attracted wider and lasting attention.[43] It showed football fans in Ukraine making Nazi salutes and violently attacking Asian fans. While the British government advised black English fans to take safety precautions in Ukraine, former England footballer Sol Campbell argued that black fans should stay at home or risk 'coming back in a coffin'. Widespread racist violence seemed inevitable at Euro 2012 as Hyper-Critical Theory would predict.

While Euronews identified racism and neo-nazis as a problem for post-Soviet football and society, they attempted to balance this with official anti-racism and liberal patriotism of ordinary fans. One bulletin explained how 'passion – for football, their club and country – turns from national pride and patriotism to xenophobia and racism' (12/06/12). A leader of the fan movement in Lviv admitted that racism exists but that it had been exaggerated by the media, even suggesting that racist violence at football is far worse in the European core:

> There is racism at matches. At all matches, whether in Ukraine or elsewhere in the world. There are some displays of it in Lviv as well. One of the reasons for this is that some youngsters confuse nationalism with racism. It's a very thin line which is all too easy to cross. Ukrainian fans mostly limit themselves to hand gestures, but in Europe – France or England – it is much worse, with beatings and killings. We don't have the same level of violence compared with the rest of Europe. (12/06/12)

In the same report, human rights activists complained that Ukraine does not collect official statistics for racially motivated violence and that the main problem is xenophobic anxiety about strangers rather than racial supremacy: 'sometimes people are hostile. It depends on how cultured they are'. Black South African students in Lviv for the football also rejected the negative characterization of Ukrainians by the British media and testified to the friendly and safe environment.

For supporters of national teams like England group charisma is more elastic than Hyper-Critical Theory allows.[44] Euronews showed England fans parading through the streets of Donetsk with a makeshift coffin to make the point that, as paraphrased by the channel's reporter, 'Sol Campbell was out of line and that the Ukraine is not a dangerous country'(19/06/12). England fans were frustrated that media fears about trouble had reduced the size of support willing to travel to Ukraine. As one supporter told Euronews: 'We've been on the streets dressed like this [Crusaders]. Nobody has caused us any problems. There has been no racism'. (19/06/12). Against images of fans and police mixing in the sunshine, the Euronews reporter suggested that only the outcome of the football game itself might sour things: 'As you can see, there's no sign of tension or violence so far, as both England and Ukrainian supporters hang out together. But maybe tonight's result will decide whether relations stay so amicable'.

A post-soviet hierarchy of football nations

In the build-up to Euro 2012, Euronews routinely positioned nations in a football hierarchy (see Figure 1). National charisma was adjusted to recent form and past experiences of defeat and victory. Some nations like England and Ukraine

Team	Assessment
Croatia	Since Slaven Bilic's arrival as coach in 2006 Croatia have not ended the year outside the top ten in the FIFA World rankings .... Since their independence the Croats have *qualified* for the European finals three times – on two of those occasions, in 1996 and 2008, they reached the quarter-finals. (30/05/12)
Czech Republic	... lost to Germany in the Euro 1996 final and reached the semi-finals in 2004, but since then have *slipped down* to 26th in the world rankings and will be eager to *re-establish themselves* as a force in European football. (08/06/12)
England	After a *disappointing* World Cup in South Africa two years ago .... England's chances at Euro 2012 have been *played down* in comparison to recent tournaments.... the only European side to have won the World Cup but never be crowned European champions. (30/05/12)
Germany	...a squad looking to end their nation's 16-year-European title *drought*. (06/06/12)
Greece	Although they were *surprise winners* in 2004, in the last edition in Austria and Switzerland, they exited the competition without a point – an *embarrassment* they will seek to make amends for on Friday. (08/06/12)
Poland	Poland are the *lowest ranked* team at the finals but they will still *fancy their chances* in group A which, on paper, appears an open contest. (08/06/12)
Portugal	the only nation out of the four *not to have won* the European championship – with Denmark victorious in 1992, Germany a three times winner (1972, 1980, 1996) while the Netherlands lifted the trophy in 1988. (06/06/12)
Spain	Reigning World and European *champions* Spain. (06/06/12)
Ukraine	Coach Oleg Blokhin ... has *no illusions* about his team's chances. (30/05/12)

Figure 1.   Position and prospects for selected teams at Euro 2012.

self-consciously lowered expectations while others like Germany and the Czech Republic looked to restore a charismatic position near the top of the football hierarchy, currently occupied by the eventual winners, Spain. Lowest ranked Poland aimed to simply improve its position and avoid group disgrace. Above all, national teams want to avoid group disgrace by occupying a satisfactory place in the hierarchy corresponding to an idea of national grace even if they cannot win the competition outright.

Here, a football hierarchy of nations operates in a perceptual universe at a remove from the geo-political hierarchy of states. As power rivals monopolizing the internal organization of violence, states represent a danger to each other. National groups continue to collectively experience the emotional extremes of national narcissism or national melancholia. If made to feel humiliated and denigrated as inferior nations may be aroused to retaliate against collective disgrace. National disgrace can be experienced personally as a loss of human value in the eyes of the world. A mood of national melancholia may follow from the feeling that present generations are failing the ancestors that once made the nation great, as in the declining football power of England or France. Alternatively, national charisma accompanies the feeling that national honour has been restored by throwing off an oppressor state, as in cases of resurgent nationalisms following the collapse of the Soviet Union, Yugoslavia and Czechoslovakia.

International football may restore to formerly oppressed post-Soviet nations a collective self-image of taking their rightful place as equals in the eyes of the world of nations. At Euro 2012, the national shame of fractured post-Soviet self-images created a desire for Ukraine to be seen as a 'normal nation' by the rest of Europe (Euronews, 08/06/12):

> 'We want to support Euro 2012 in Ukraine and to show people from Europe that we are just like they are; that there are no bears walking on the streets of Kyiv but normal and decent people, who are always glad to meet friends and guests who come to visit'.

At the start of the competition, an upsurge of national prestige was reported as a consequence of Ukraine becoming the focal point of a global audience: 'I am proud of Ukraine because we organized Euro 2012 very well' (02/07/12). Quoting the Mayor of Lviv, Euronews claimed:

> Ukrainian people are getting used to a lovely and slightly unusual feeling. The feeling of pride. 'Pride. Pride for Lviv. Pride for our native country. It's a special feeling that sends shivers down the spine, when tears appear. And you want so much to have this pride permanently' (26/06/12)

At Euro 2012, the strengthened we-image produced by the globalizing figuration appeared to draw Ukrainian nationalism closer to the ideals of European culture, tastes and values. This positive image of Ukrainian hospitality was repeatedly reinforced by Euronews bulletins:

> Most foreign fans were pleasantly surprized when they arrived in Ukraine, as the media back home had prepared them for much worse … In the end they're delighted with the country they discovered for themselves. Friendship between Ukrainian and foreign fans can be seen everywhere, and the Euro has not only been a great time for visitors, but for locals as well. (25/06/12)

> the festivities and songs in all the different languages are heard throughout streets of the host cities, and the party goes on. (25/06/12)

As one Euro volunteer said, 'Euro has opened a new page for Lviv. We have rubbed out the stereotype of the post-Soviet country' (26/06/12).

Official fan-zones and cultural events were organized in public spaces (08/06/12).[45] In Kiev's fan-zone workshops were held for folk-crafts and local cooking, alongside hours of live music, often performed in English, the global language of commercial culture. One electro-pop band interviewed by Euronews, Gorchitza, declared their mainly English influences 'giving their music a real European feel', and reached for well-worn cultural stereotypes to legitimate collective self-images: 'Some say Ukrainians are like the Irish: hot-tempered, explosive, but really kind' (29/05/12). 'Normal' nations must also possess their own unique 'folk traditions', as the media coordinator of a Ukrainian folk revival festival told Euronews: 'It's like Euro 2012's cultural capital. We are trying to combine culture and football and, I think, this is absolutely normal' (22/06/12). One Ukrainian fan added: 'Don't think that football fans are just beer-lovers, people who are not interested in culture, who have just one interest – football. We also love world music, we respect our traditions and we're interested in the work of folk artists' (22/06/12).

Group charisma from hosting the competition was transformed into national euphoria when the Ukraine 'minority of 11' unexpectedly beat Sweden in their first game. Euronews put transitory national sporting success in economic and political context: 'an entire nation whose attention has been temporarily diverted from the country's economic problems and political tension' (14/06/12). One Ukrainian summed up the effect: 'During the matches, people forget all their troubles. You just worry about the game, about Ukraine, the coach and the players' (15/06/12). Political divisions between ethnic Ukrainians and the large minority of Russian Ukrainians were briefly overcome. As a Ukrainian journalist argued:

> When the Russian team plays, we can see a divide of two countries here, two societies. In Lviv, people will shout 'Hurray! Here it goes!' when the Russian team loses, and in Donetsk, they would celebrate every goal scored by Russia. But when it comes to the Ukrainian team, everyone unites behind them. (15/06/12)

Such sentiments echo the founding ideology of UEFA as a depoliticized zone of unity, overcoming internal ethnic divisions.

The agony, the ecstasy and the score-draw

> Then Ronaldo struck, prompting jubilation. (22/06/12)

> Crowds in Madrid … saw the fans erupt each time the ball hit the back of the Italian net. (01/07/12)

> Wonderful. Unforgettable. Having won like this is wonderful. We deserved even more goals, but it was great anyway. (Italian fan, 29/06/12)

Football not only stimulates cathartic release in an absolute moment of triumph. Pleasure is also taken in the tension and deferral of gratification by the game-contest itself. International football allows for a ritualistic re-enactment of old enmities but also allows for the relief of new tensions. In football, therefore, class resentment or nationalist tensions do not possess the same force of seriousness that they might have in a more directly political or economic context. A demonstration of skill on the football pitch can re-route economic and political tensions between nations in controlled directions, lessening rather than exacerbating the prospects for mass nationalist violence.

> 'We rather prefer Germany,' said one Spanish fan. 'It's because technically I think we are better than them. And above all because if Mrs Merkel cuts us off economically, we will cut them off on the pitch'. (28/06/12)

Football itself creates tensions and excites violent emotions in socially approved ways. So long as specific limits are observed, fans may indulge in the vicarious experience of collective hatred and the desire to humiliate rivals without breaking out into serious violence. Within football symbolic violence is socially approved, while unrestrained physical violence rarely is.

Even within the limits of the Euronews format an attempt was made to convey something of the tension-balance within games. Reports relied on judgements about technical superiority ('clinical', 'dominated', 'thrash', 'convincing win', 'class', 'precision', etc.) and physical exertion ('determined', 'frustrating', 'effort', 'struggled', 'held on', 'edge out', etc.) (see Figure 2). Some games were dramatic and exciting, tipping towards the excitement pole, while games that were tense, narrow affairs lean towards the boredom pole, as do games that are so one-sided that there is little tension or competition to be enjoyed. In line with most football reporting, Euronews concentrated on moments of high spectacle – the excitement pole – individual skill, goals and dramatic changes in play but was also compelled to represent the boredom pole, for instance in tactically narrow contests where attacking play is largely cancelled out in tense stalemates. Tension is further stimulated by the foresight and calculation demanded by the points format of the competition at the group qualifying stages, followed by the drama of knock-out rounds and penalty shoot-outs, where, at any moment, a mistake or display of skill can prove decisive.

Defeat without disgrace

International football is less 'playful' and more 'serious' than leisure football. The 'best minority of 11' perform a representative function for the self-images of national charisma, more accurately, the wish-image national constructions of sports journalism. At top-level international competitions, cathartic resolution is constantly deferred in the face of inevitable setbacks and defeats in the hierarchy of competing football nations. International football is as much, or even more so, the occasion of national anguish within a spoiled mimesis as it is for national self-praise in the cathartic resolution of outright victory.

Every national team, except one (Spain in Euro 2012), will lose at some point. National we-images are therefore forced to adjust to the reality of impending defeat. International football provides training in collective self-restraint at the same time as it excites nationalist emotions. All nations experience defeat on the playing field, moderating, if not eliminating, fantasy images of the national we-group by reality images of the skill, chance, probabilities, tactics, organization, and so on of rival teams. Even national rivalries established at earlier phases of the state formation process, such as between England and France or Germany and the Netherlands, tend to be resolved with equanimity, more or less, despite contrasting emotions.

> There were cheers and shouts of joy from jubilant German football fans, but misery and dejection from supporters of the Netherlands. Germany's 2:1 win in the European Championships against their long term rivals sparked a night of celebration – for some. (14/06/12)

After the opening match ended in a draw, Poles and Greeks leaving the stadium praised each other. As one Greek fan put it, 'the result is fair ... Polish people are very nice people, they are very good people' (09/06/12). Fans were shown as being stoic in defeat, if anything turning inwards for the causes of defeat rather than resenting the victors.

Date	Result	Report
9 June	Poland 1 Greece 1	Lewandowski *thrilled* the home fans opening up the scoring equalizing *against the flow of play* and silencing the home crowd
9 June	Netherlands v Denmark	Denmark pulled off the first *big surprise* of the tournament with an *impressive* 1-0 win over the Netherlands
9 June	Russia 4 Czech Republic 1	The Russian team got off to *a flying start*
10 June	Germany 1 Poland 0	Germany *edge out* Portugal a *narrow* 1-0 win
11 June	Ukraine 2 Sweden 1	a *thrilling* 2-1 win
11 June	Croatia 3 Ireland 1	Croatia played with *class and precision* Slaven Bilic's team played with an *energy and directness*
11 June	Spain 1 Italy 1	tournament favourites Spain were held to a *frustrating* 1-1 draw by a *determined* Italian side.
12 June	Czech Republic 2 Greece 1	the 2004 champions were unable to salvage a point against a *determined* Czech side
12 June	Poland 1 Russia 1	Group A favourites Russia were held to a *frustrating* 1-1 draw by co-hosts Poland
12 June 2102	Ukraine 2 Sweden 1	Ukraine's Euro 2012 party started in *style*
12 June	Portugal 3 Denmark 2	In a *thrilling* ending to the match Portugal's attacking *pressure* paid off
13 June	Poland 1 Russia 1	To the delight of the home fans Poland had *dominated* the early exchanges at the National Stadium. But on 37 minutes Polish delight turned to *agony*… With the hopes of a nation weighing heavily on their shoulders Poland *stepped it up* a notch in the second half – and their *efforts* soon paid dividends.
14 June	Spain 4 Ireland 0	a *solid* performance for Vicente del Bosque's men
14 June	Italy 1 Croatia 1	*Italy*… started the encounter *brightly* Croatia refused to sit back and gradually *forced* their way back into the tie
14 June	Germany 2 Netherlands 1	Germany gave the Dutch a lesson in *clinical* football
16 June	Greece 1 Russia 0	2004 champions Greece *stunned* Group A favourites Russia Despite Russia *dominating* the majority of play… midfielder Giorgos Karagounis's first half stoppage-time goal gave Greece a *dramatic* and *surprise* victory

Figure 2.   Excitement and boredom in Euronews reports of Euro 2012.

16 June	Czech Republic 1 Poland 0	The Czech Republic qualified for the quarter-finals … in a *dramatic* final round of matches in group A.
16 June	England 3 Sweden 2	England and their fans breathed a sigh of *relief* at Euro 2012 on Friday night after they came from behind to beat Sweden 3-2
16 June	France 2 Ukraine 0	the win the French *desperately* needed
19 June	Italy 2 Ireland 0	a *convincing* 2-0 win over the Republic of Ireland
19 June	Spain 1 Croatia 0	Vicente del Bosque's men *dominated* possession and eventually scored the goal they needed two minutes from time
20 June	France 0 Sweden 2	Les Bleus *missed* too many opportunities in front of goal and conceded an *outstanding* second half goal courtesy of Zlatan Ibrahimovic.
20 June	England 1 Ukraine 0	Roy Hodgson's men *held on* to their lead and *just did enough* to secure all three points
21 June	Czech Republic 0 Portugal 1	Portugal *dominated*, but the Czechs were kept in the game by several *fine saves* from keeper Petr Cech.
23 June	Germany 4 Greece 2	It was a bit of a *frustrating* opening half an hour for the Germans who *struggled* with *wasteful* finishing and *sloppy* passes.
24 June	Spain 2 France 0	Jordi Alba brought life to an otherwise *unspectacular* game
25 June	England 2 Italy 4 (on pens)	England *survived* wave after wave of attack from the Italians, who apart from the first five minutes of the match *dominated* regulation and added time
28 June	Italy 2 Germany 1	Balotelli *shines* as Italy beat Germany to reach final
1 July	Spain 4 Italy 0	Spain *thrash* Italy 4-0 to retain European crown

Figure 2. (*Continued*)

The Scandinavians [Sweden] surprised locals, maintaining a cheerful mood despite losing 2 – 1 to the host country. (25/06/12)

It looks like the Netherlands' supporters do not know the meaning of misery. (25/06/12)

'I'm not too sad because the Portuguese team played very well'. (Losing Portuguese fan, 28/06/12)

'We're obviously disappointed after the defeat. We would like to have won, but what's most important is the experience of being in Ukraine to support the French national team and that's an unforgettable moment!'. (Losing French fan, 24/06/12)

'The Italians played well, we must admit that'. (Losing German fan, 29/06/12)

'The Spanish deserved to win, though not 4–0'. (Losing Italian fan, 02/07/12)

Euronews daily repeated an image of good losers and peaceful contact between fans. Before the final an Italian fan was interviewed: 'The Spanish and ourselves are like brothers. In Kiev everything's OK. We say hello to each other, exchange pictures, because after all football is important but it's not the end of the world' (01/07/12). Some fans exemplified their nation's self-image of charismatic conviviality whatever the result:

> For football fans visiting Euro 2012, it is not only about what happens on the pitch. It is also a chance to enjoy the festivities around the games. While Irish supporters were stealing the show in Poland, Swedish fans were trying to bring similar joy to Ukraine's capital, Kiev. (25/06/12)

Because it is bound up with collective self-images of nationhood, built-up tensions may *not* be resolved at the final whistle. As we have noted, players and supporters may still 'go over the score' and transgress the boundaries placed on approved forms of symbolic violence should the national team lose or be disgraced in some way. At Euro 2012 this proved something of an exception rather than the rule.

Conclusion

For the organizers of international competitions like UEFA, sport potentially represents a depoliticized autonomous field of universal interdependency between nations, where all that matters is the game itself being played within certain limits of approved conduct. From detailed study of Euronews reports, Euro 2012 fostered a dynamic, cross-national, post-Soviet figuration rather than simply furthering the interests of commercialized sport and militarism anticipated by Hyper-Critical Theory.[46] By positing a categorical negation of the official football ideology as universal (particular), civilizing (alienating), purifying (corrupting) and elevating (stultifying), Hyper-Critical Theory effectively abandoned the utopian moment of the repressed desires that football figurations like Euro 2012 expresses.

In a context of heightened state rivalries, institutional crisis and national chauvinism across Europe, the incipient violence inherent to the 'sport mode of production' ought to have led to 'unrestrained, generalized violence' at Euro 2012 predicted by Hyper-Critical Theory. There was no generalised violence. The behaviour of players, officials and spectators was generally restrained, despite reports of some episodes of nationalist and racist abuse and fighting between rival fans. Instead of focussing on exceptional moments of unrestrained violence what needs explained instead is the routine collective and personal control over fluctuating emotional tensions at football matches.[47] Euro 2012 functioned generally as a 'symbolic representation of non-violent, non-military competition between states'.[48] Although a number of violent incidents were reported at Euro 2012 by Euronews, the formal threshold for on-field violence has been raised to a historically high level. An illustration of this is that the number of cautions and dismissals at Euro 2012 remained at the historically low level of Euro 2008. Football effects a temporary release from self-restraint, 'a controlled decontrolling of restraint' not possible in other spheres of daily life. Here, the seriousness of international football competitions suggests a converging tendency of 'sportization' between nations.

Outside of wartime, competitions like Euro 2012 offer one of the few venues for the group charisma of post-Soviet nations to find a global public at a definite, crisis-ridden phase in the state formation process. Even now, in the depths of decay and crisis, this does not always demand victory at all costs. Rather, the development of national charisma establishes self-images of the 'national game', where it is understood that certain, albeit changeable practices of fans or players demean or shame the nation in the eyes of a global football public, while other practices earn respect and recognition. No social group, players, officials, media or fans, is able to disregard entirely the field capabilities of the 'best minority of 11' engaged in the serious game of exemplifying group charisma.

Acknowledgements

The author acknowledges the critical insight and helpful suggestions of Christos Memos and Peter Kennedy on an earlier version of this paper.

Notes

1. http://www.uefa.com/uefaeuro/abouteuro/organisation/logobrand/index.html.
2. Smith, *Globalization*.
3. Just weeks before Euro 2012 Jürgen Fitschen, joint head of Germany's biggest bank, Deutsche, reportedly described Greece as 'a failed state ... a corrupt state'. In an interview with the *Guardian* newspaper, Christine Lagarde, Managing Director of the IMF, was reported as having more sympathy for victims of poverty in sub-Saharan Africa than Greeks hit by the economic crisis. Elliot and Aitkenhead, 'It's payback time'.
4. Mittag and Benjamin, 'Towards a Europeanization of Football', 720.
5. Inthorn, 'Europe divided, or Europe united?'; Crolley, Hand and Jeutter. 'Playing the Identity Card'; King, 'Football Fandom and Post-national Identity in the New Europe'; Maguire, and Poulton. 'European Identity Politics in Euro 96'; Poulton, 'Mediated Patriot Games'.
6. Kaptyken, *The Stateless Market*, 142.
7. Morrissey, 'Un homme avant tout'.
8. The eleven languages are: Arabic, English, French, German, Italian, Persian, Portuguese, Russian, Spanish, Turkish, and Ukrainian.
9. Gripsrud, 'Television and the European Public Sphere'.
10. Garcia-Blanco and Cushion, 'A Partial Europe Without Citizens or EU-level Political Institutions'.
11. Billig, *Banal Nationalism*.
12. 'EURO 2012™ broadcasting deal agreed with EBU', 23 September 2009, http://www.uefa.com/uefa/mediaservices/mediareleases/newsid=941165.html.
13. The European Championship alternates with FIFA's World Cup for a share of the global sports-media audience. Even more nations will participate as the competition expands from 16 to 24 teams for Euro 2016 in France. Plans for multiple host countries across Europe for Euro 2020 met early opposition in a survey of fans. See James Riach, 'Fans Reject Michel Platini's "zany" Plan for Continent-wide Euro 2020', *The Guardian*, 7 December 2012.
14. Euro 2012, *Regulations of the UEFA European Football Championship*, 49.
15. Ibid., 51.
16. Ibid., 51.

17. Ibid., 52, emphasis added.
18. Wiggerhaus, Rolf, *The Frankfurt School*.
19. Adorno, 'Veblen's Attack on Culture', 81.
20. Rigauer, *Sport and Work*.
21. Perelman, *Barbaric Sport*, 48.
22. Perelman, *Barbaric Sport*, 43.
23. Perelman, *Barbaric Sport*, 33, emphasis added.
24. Ibid., 22.
25. Brohm, *Sport, A Prison of Measured Time*, 15.
26. Hargreaves, *Sport, Power and Culture*; Gruneau, 'The Critique of Sport in Modernity'.
27. Morgan, 'Adorno on Sport'. For a liberal reconstruction of Critical Theory of sport see Morgan, *Leftist Theories of Sport*.
28. Inglis, 'Theodor Adorno on Sport'.
29. Elias, 'Address on Adorno'.
30. Elias and Dunning, *Quest for Excitement*. For a survey of figurational studies and debates in the sociology of sport see Liston, 'Sport and Leisure'.
31. Elias, 'An Essay on Sport and Violence'. For a global sociological history of football see Goldblatt, *The Ball is Round*.
32. Elias, Norbert, 'Group Charisma and Group Disgrace'; Elias, 'A Theoretical Essay on Established and Outsider Relations'.
33. Elias and Dunning, 'Dynamics of Sport Groups with Special References to Football, 200–03; Elias, Introduction, Note 11, 287–9.
34. Elias and Dunning, 'Leisure in the Spare-time Spectrum', 125.
35. Elias, Introduction, Note 11, 289.
36. Elias, 'Introduction', 44.
37. Perelman, *Barbaric Sport*, 34.
38. Brohm, *Sport, a Prison of Measured Time*, 180.
39. Zolberg, 'Elias and Dunning's Theory of Sport and Excitement'.
40. Dunning, *Sport Matters*, 111.
41. Giulianotti, 'Civilizing Games'.
42. Dunning, 'Figurational Sociology and the Sociology of Sport'.
43. http://www.bbc.co.uk/news/uk-18192375.
44. Gibbons, 'English National Identity and the National Football Team'.
45. Lauss and Szigetvari, 'Governing by Fun'.
46. Manzenreiter and Spitaler, 'Governance, Citizenship and the New European Football Championships'.
47. Elias, 'Football in the Process of Civilisation'.
48. Elias, 'Introduction', 23.

References

Adorno, Theodor W. 'Veblen's Attack on Culture'. In *Prisms*, 73–94. Cambridge, MA: MIT Press, 1967.
Billig, Michael. *Banal Nationalism*. London: Sage, 1995.
Brohm, Jean-Marie. *Sport: A Prison of Measured Time*, London: Pluto Press, 1978.
Crolley, L., D. Hand, and R. Jeutter. 'Playing the Identity Card: Stereotypes in European Football'. *Soccer & Society* 1 (2000): 107–28.
Dunning, Eric. *Sport Matters: Sociological Studies of Sport, Violence and Civilization*, London: Routledge, 1999.
Dunning, Eric 'Figurational Sociology and the Sociology of Sport: Some Concluding Remarks'. In *Sport and Leisure in the Civilizing Process: Critique and Counter-Critique*, ed. E. Dunning and C. Rojek, 221–84. Basingstoke: Macmillan, 1992.
Elias, Norbert and Eric, Dunning. 'Leisure in the Spare-time Spectrum'. In *Quest for Excitement: Sport and Leisure in the Civilizing Process*. Oxford: Basil Blackwell, 1986.
Elias, Norbert, and Eric Dunning. *Quest for Excitement: Sport and Leisure in the Civilizing Process*, 91–125. Oxford: Basil Blackwell, 1986.

Elias, Norbert. 'A Theoretical Essay on Established and Outsider Relations'. In *The Established and the Outsiders*, ed. Norbert Elias and John L. Scotston, xv–lii. London: Sage, 1994.

Elias, Norbert. 'An Essay on Sport and Violence'. In *Quest for Excitement: Sport and Leisure in the Civilizing Process*, 150–74. Oxford: Basil Blackwell, 1986.

Elias, Norbert. 'Processes of State Formation and Nation-building'. In *Collected Works*, Vol. 15, ed. R. Kilminster and S. Mennell, 105–18. Dublin: University College Dublin Press, 2008.

Elias, Norbert. 'Group Charisma and Group Disgrace'. In *Collected Works*, Vol. 16, ed. R. Kilminster and S. Mennell, 73–81. Dublin: University College Dublin Press, 2009.

Elias, Norbert. 'Football in the Process of Civilisation'. In *Collected Works*, Vol. 16, ed. R. Kilminster and S. Mennell, 190–97. Dublin: University College Dublin Press, 2009.

Elias, Norbert .'Address on Adorno: Respect and Critique'. In *Collected Works*, Vol. 16, ed. R. Kilminster and S. Mennell, 82–91. Dublin: University College Dublin Press, 2009.

Elliot, Larry. and Decca, Aitkenhead. 'It's Payback Time: Don't Expect Sympathy – Lagarde to Greeks', *The Guardian*, May 25, 2012.

Euro 2012. *Regulations of the UEFA European Football Championship, 2010–12*, 2009. http://www.uefa.com/MultimediaFiles/Download/Regulations/competitions/Regulations/91/48/36/914836_DOWNLOAD.pdf.

Garcia-Blanco, Inaki, and Stephen Cushion. 'A Partial Europe Without Citizens or EU-level Political Institutions'. *Journalism Studies* 11 (2010): 393–411.

Georg, Lauss, and András Szigetvari. 'Governing by Fun: EURO 2008 and the Appealing Power of Fan Zones'. *Soccer & Society* 11, no. 6 (2010): 737–47.

Gibbons, Tom. 'English National Identity and the National Football Team: The View of Contemporary English Fans'. *Soccer & Society* 12, no. 6 (2011): 865–79.

Giulianotti, Richard. 'Civilizing games: Norbert Elias and the Sociology of Sport'. In *Sport and Modern Social Theorists*, ed. R. Giulianotti, 145–60. Basingstoke: Palgrave Macmillan, 2004.

Goldblatt, David. *The Ball is Round: A Global History of Football*, London: Penguin, 2007.

Gripsrud, Jorstein. 'Television and the European Public Sphere'. *European Journal of Communications* 22 (2007): 479–92.

Gruneau, Richard. 'The Critique of Sport in Modernity: Theorising Power, Culture and the Politics of the Body'. In *The Sports Process: A Comparative and Developmental Approach*, ed. Eric G. Dunning, Joseph A. Maguire and Robert E. Pearton, 85–110. Champaign, IL: Human Kinetics, 1993.

Hargreaves, John. *Sport, Power and Culture*. Oxford: Polity Press, 1986.

Inglis, David. 'Theodor Adorno on Sport: The *jeu d'esprit* of Despair'. In *Sport and Modern Social Theorists*, ed. R. Giulianotti, 81–96. Palgrave Macmillan: Basingstoke, 2004.

Inthorn, Sanna. 'Europe Divided, or Europe United? German and British Press Coverage of the 2008 European Championship'. *Soccer & Society* 11, no. 6 (2010): 790–802.

Kaptyken, Paul. *The Stateless Market: The European Dilemma of Integration and Civilization*, London: Routledge, 1996.

King, Anthony. 'Football Fandom and Post-national Identity in the New Europe'. *British Journal of Sociology* 51 (2000): 419–42.

Liston, Kate 'Sport and Leisure'. In *Norbert Elias and Figurational Research: Processual Thinking in Sociology*, ed. N. Gabriel and S. Mennell, 160–80. Oxford: Wiley-Blackwell/The Sociological Review, 2011.

Maguire, Joseph, and Emma Poulton. 'European Identity Politics in Euro 96: Invented Traditions and National Habitus Codes'. *International Review for the Sociology of Sport* 34 (1999): 17–29.

Manzenreiter, Wolfram, and Georg Spitaler. 'Governance, Citizenship and the New European Football Championships: The European Spectacle'. *Soccer & Society* 11, no. 6 (2010): 695–708.

Mittag, Jürgen, and Benjamin Legrand. 'Towards a Europeanization of Football: Historical Phases in the Evolution of the UEFA European Football Championship'. *Soccer & Society* 11, no. 6 (2010): 709–22.

Morgan, William J. 'Adorno on Sport: The Case of the Fractured Dialectic'. *Theory and Society* 17, no. 6 (1988): 818–38.

Morgan, William J. *Leftist Theories of Sport: A Critique and Reconstruction*, Champaign, IL: University of Illinois Press, 1994.

Morrissey, Sean. "Un homme avant tout': Zinedine Zidane and the Sociology of a Head-butt'. *Soccer & Society* 10, no. 2 (2009): 210–25.

Perelman, Marc. *Barbaric Sport: A Global Plague*, London: Verso, 2012.

Poulton, Emma. 'Mediated Patriot Games: The Construction and Representation of National Identities in the British Television Production of Euro'96'. *International Review for the Sociology of Sport* 39 (2004): 437–55.

Rigauer, Bero. *Sport and Work*, New York: Columbia University Press, 1981.

Smith, Dennis. *Globalization: The Hidden Agenda*, Cambridge: Polity Press, 2006.

Wiggerhaus, Rolf. *The Frankfurt School: Its History, Theory and Political Significance*, Cambridge: Polity, 1995.

Zolberg, Vera. 'Elias and Dunning's Theory of Sport and Excitement'. *Theory, Culture and Society* 4, no. 2–3 (1987): 571–75.

'They think it's all Dover!' Popular newspaper narratives and images about the English football team and (re)presentations of national identity during Euro 2012

John Vincent[a] and John Harris[b]

[a]Department of Kinesiology, The University of Alabama, Tuscaloosa, USA; [b]Department of Business Management, Glasgow Caledonian University, Glasgow, Scotland

The 2012 UEFA European Football Championship ('Euro 2012') – Europe's quadrennial football bonanza was held in Poland and the Ukraine between June 8th and July 1st. Occurring between Elizabeth II's Diamond jubilee and the London 2012 Olympic Games, the eyes of the media were fixated on the pride and joy of English football, its men's national team. With national consciousness at an all-time high, articles in England's tabloid, 'red-top,' daily national newspapers *The Sun* and *Daily Mirror* were tracked for three weeks as they lavished their attentions on the national pastime. Their coverage of the English team reflected a heightened consciousness of English national identity. Drawing on Guibernau's strategies for creating and uniting citizens around a collective national identity, this study examined how England's popular media presented and represented England's national identity to reflect the real and imagined versions of Englishness during this major sporting event.[1] By focusing on *The Sun and Daily Mirror*'s narratives about, and images of, the English team during the Euro 2012 tournament, this paper focuses on how English national identity ebbed and flowed during a time of seismic change within the country. Shaped by an inductive textual analysis, this paper shows how the press fluctuated between optimistic notions of the present and future English national identity and traditional 'olde England' in an almost formulaic fashion.

Introduction

The summer in 2012 was a hectic time for the English and British press with the patriotic pomp and pagentry of the Queen's Diamond Jubilee celebrations and the much anticipated London 2012 Olympic Games. In the midst of an economic downturn and still reeling from the government's recently imposed austerity measures, Britain was in a state of flux as government spending cuts had caused civil unrest, rioting, and looting in several major cities in England the previous summer. Additionally, there were further pressures with the Eurozone debt crisis, the push for Scottish independence, and the potential break-up of the UK.

In some ways then, English identity was in crisis, torn between the Little Englander, Eurosceptic mindset, and its global counterpart that was hosting the Olympic Games, the world's premier athletic sporting event. The alternatives were clear: it was either old traditional England or a global England that welcomed the world's nations to London. There was a sense of relief among England's sport columnists that the Euro 2012 football championship took place over June and July in Poland and the Ukraine. Torn between a past as a stand-alone nation and its future as part of the European and world communities, the English press had a clear decision to make during Euro 2012: should it revert back to its old 'England first' rhetoric or demonstrate its global statesmanship through commentaries more befitting its alternative citizen of the world image?

Muddying the waters further, immediately prior to Euro 2012, there had been a 'war of words' between Britain and France over the encroaching powers of the European Union into British affairs. Given that England's first game in Euro 2012 was against France, this added an extra twist to the usual competitive ambience.

This study examines how two tabloid 'red-top' English newspapers, *The Sun* and the *Daily Mirror*, covered the English national football team in the 2012 UEFA European Football Championships. Whilst it is important to note that these publications may promote a particular form of English identity, the fact that they are amongst the best-selling daily newspapers in the country means that the images (re)presented are read by a sizeable audience. We first identify and delineate the role of national identity as a fluid cultural construct and then deconstruct it into its specific geopolitical and socio-historical contexts to provide a snapshot analysis of English identity during this time of seismic change in Britain.

National identity and international football

Guibernau defined national identity as '[a] collective sentiment based upon the belief of belonging to the same nation and sharing most of the attributes that make it distinct from other nations'.[2] National identity can comprise many dimensions, including a demarcated geographical territory, a common language, a shared sense of historical connection, continuity, and culture, and commonly held myths, symbols, and values that distinguish it from other national identities. Thus, national identity unites citizens by evoking a shared collective sense of belonging and consciousness that focus on the unique national attributes, traditions, values, and symbols. Reinforced in the collective ingrained memory or habitus of its citizens, the tenets of national identity receive further bolstering through the discourses of politicians, historians, and journalists. As such, as Parekh articulated, national identity is not fixed, but is rather a social construction which is fluid, dynamic, and open '… to unlimited construction'.[3] Anderson and Hobsbawm both add their weight to the notion that national identity is constantly evolving and may be re-imagined or re-invented within contemporary contexts.[4,5]

Cultural studies scholar Stuart Hall noted how 'all of us are composed of multiple social identities'.[6] Although collective identities such as gender, class, and race all coexist and intersect, national identity is perceived to be a unifying aspect for most people within a country.[7] Indeed, as Guibernau posited,

> … individuals identify with and … regard as their own the accomplishments of their fellow nationals. It is by identifying with the nation that individuals' finite lives are transcended and that the nation comes to be revered as a higher entity. One of the most outstanding features of national identity is its ability to cut across class divisions while strengthening a sentiment of belonging to an artificial type of extended family, the nation.[8]

With the exception of war, nowhere is this sense of national unity, consciousness, and belonging more prevalent than in the context of major international sporting competitions. This is particularly true for England and English football. As Hobsbawm articulated, 'the imagined community of millions seems more real as a team of eleven named people'.[9] Similarily, Giulianotti reflected that during an international football tournament popular expressions of nationalism override all other considerations with – the nation often literally wrapping itself in the national flag'.[10] These popular expressions of nationalism become important because as von der Lippe noted, national identity is defined by 'how a citizenry sees and thinks about themselves in relations to others'.[11] This contrast in cultural national identity is reflected in media accounts about international sporting contests.

The 'sport-nationalism-media troika'

Rowe et al. described the interface between national teams, the media, and their audiences as the 'sport-nationalism-media troika'.[12] The media play an important role in shaping, (re)producing, and reflecting a shared national cultural consciousness during major international sporting competitions.[13] Hunter noted how the competition and drama of international sporting tournaments provide newspapers through prose and photographs the opportunity to evoke strong emotions and nationalist sentiments.[14]

Vincent and Hill chronicled how *the Sun's* coverage of the 2010 FIFA World Cup in South Africa not only covered the performance of the English national team but also the antics and behaviors of their 'army' of supporters, complete with their carnivalesque reenactments of English pageantry, traditions, and rituals.[15] These expressions of Englishness provided the media journalists with rich emotive materials to generate interest and mobilize support to allow their readership through the newspapers' narratives and images to 'be there' and share the championship atmosphere and experiences through the 'imagined community' back in the homeland. In line with *The Sun's* sensationalist approach, their journalists adroitly and creatively captured graphic accounts of supporters' off-the-field cultural recreation and performances, replete with emotive rhetoric, language, and the inventive use of metaphors, similies, metonyms, double entendres, and headline puns. All were designed to entertain and evoke support from their 'imagined community' of readers.

English identity and football

'Two world wars and a world cup'

Historian Richard Weight articulated how at the beginning of the 21st century, English identity was still inextricably intertwined with British identity.[16] This included two world wars and the nation's 'finest hour' in standing alone against the Nazi tyranny of the Second World War. He further noted that much changed in the two decades that followed the Second World War as the financial exertions of those wars resulted in post-war austerity punctuated by gradual economic decline. This, coupled with the gradual loss of the empire, resulted in a downturn in global confidence and influence. In part this was offset by a golden age in English popular culture during the 'swinging sixties.' It was a time when English popular music, headlined by the Beatles, the Rolling Stones, and the Who dominated the radio airwaves. London's Carnaby Street became the fashion center of the world, and Ian Fleming's James Bond captivated global cinema audiences. To cap off this golden era, the English national football team won the 1966 World Cup, beating World War II nemesis

West Germany in the final at Wembley stadium. This was heralded as English sports 'finest hour'.

Evoking the Orwellian notion of international sport as 'war minus the shooting', Weight recalled how after defeating Germany in two wars, England's World Cup victory against West Germany '… mutually reinforced war and football in the English mind' in 'us vs. them' narratives.[17] On the eve of the final, Weight recalled how the *Daily Mail* reinforced the divisive 'us vs. them' tensions by stating, 'If Germany beat us at Wembley this afternoon at our national sport, we can always point out to them that we have recently beaten them twice at theirs'.[18] The favorable outcome produced an outpouring of sports patriotism comparable to the Victory in Europe celebrations. From 1966 onwards the English national football team's success or failure became a symbol of England's health as a nation.[19,20]

Football's coming home

After 'thirty years of hurt' in which England failed to repeat the triumph of 1966, England hosted the EURO tournament in 1996. In a series of studies examining English newspaper discourses of the tournament, Maguire and colleagues found that English national identity was still largely defined by the Second World War and the 1966 World Cup victory.[21,22,23] Copious references were made to England's 'finest hour' to evoke the ingrained habitus of wartime national unity. Equally fabled was the World Cup victory of the 'boys of '66' that was recalled, re-imagined, and re-popularized in the lyrics of the English football team's Euro '96 anthem, *Three Lions*, which topped the popular music charts during the tournament. It nostalgically celebrated the exploits of three English lions from '66, Bobby Moore, Bobby Charlton, and Nobby Stiles. The song lamented, in a half serious but half joking way, England's failure to repeat their success of '66, while daring to dream that it could be repeated.

On the eve of the Euro '96 semifinal match between England and Germany the 'red-top' newspapers focused on 'us vs. them' rhetoric, replete with military metaphors. Typifying this was the *Daily Mirror's* editor Piers Morgan's declaration of 'football war on Germany' and a front page headline set against head shots of two English players, Paul Gascoigne and Stuart Pearce, with superimposed army helmets, which read 'ACTUNG! SURRENDER: For you Fritz, ze Euro 96 Championship is over' (*Daily Mirror*, 24 June 1996, Front Page).

Vincent et al. examined English newspaper coverage of the 2006 World Cup, forty years on from the success of 1966, and found that the myths of English football's 'finest hour' still resonated throughout newspaper narratives.[24] At the outset of the tournament an 'England expects' optimistic mood permeated the English newspapers headlines, columns, and images. However, the build-them-up mood of national euphoria was followed by the all too predictable knock-them-down press cycle as the English team was eliminated on penalties at the quarter-final stage. A journalistic national inquest began that included vitriolic criticism and negative stereotypes heaped on an easy foreign scapegoat, England's Swedish manager, Sven-Göran Eriksson.[25]

The contradictions of English national identity

Britain was formed by the Act of Union in 1707 between England and Scotland. Politically it cemented English hegemony over the Celtic nations and for the next

300 years, the British and English identities were largely synonymous.[26,27] However, by the end of the 20th century with the British Empire all but extinct, England struggled with its post-imperial identity.[28] This sparked, as Pocock articulated, a resurgence of the English identity.[29] 'Englishness' moods elevated as Scotland made moves for separation and the European Union gained strength. It was part of a 20th century decline that many English national identity scholars had chronicled as Britain fell from an imperial hegemonic power to middle-ranking European power.[30,31,32,33] With a devalued national self-image, England and the English increasingly began, as Gervais noted, to live back to a time when 'Britannia ruled the waves'.[34] It was an infinitely preferable mindset to the reality of a Britain that was falling apart with devolution and a Europe whose actions were increasingly dictated by EU superpower Germany.

In search of a New Jerusalem – re-imaging a new identity

In the *Break-up of Britain*, Tom Nairn first outlined the possibility of an Englishness that had regressed back to the era of its imperial heritage. Nairn pointed out that English identity had traditionally rested on the patrician influence and the stability of its constitutional and parliamentary system. Nairn critiqued the English class system of 'government by gentlemen' which stifled the equality required for popular nationalism to prosper and flourish.[35]

Ingelbien suggested that a new English identity provided an opportunity to forge a post-imperial identity which would embrace the new multi-cultural reality.[36] Weight re-imagined a post-Britain English identity based on its cultural strengths of popular music, fashion, and football, with the latter '… a more popular source of patriotism than religion'.[37] This new identity would embrace ethnicity, as Aughey suggested that the English football team, which contained many men of color, could provide a progressive model for popular English inclusiveness and diversity.[38] However, left wing social activists like Billy Bragg, have suggested that a liberal, inclusive, multicultural, and patriotic Englishness would upset the balance and at least in the short-term be unacceptable to traditional supporters that include xenophobic, violent hooligans that disrespected and abused the racial and ethnic diversity motive at World Cup and Euro tournaments. It found media expression in the outrage and public anxiety caused by home-grown, radical Moslems in the terrorist bombings in London on 7 July 2005.

Theoretical considerations

This examination of media narratives and images about English national identity during the Euro 2012 tournament drew on Guibernau's strategies to mobilize and reaffirm a collective national identity and Hobsbawm's[39] theory of invented traditions. Guibernau articulated how the media have the power to frame and disseminate "…a particular 'image of the nation', replete with '… symbols and rituals, values, principles, traditions and ways of life, and common enemies, and, even more crucially, a clear-cut definition of what constitutes a 'good citizen'"[40] (This is a direct quote from Guibernau, 2007, p. 25). Guibernau outlined four strategies that perpetuated the sense of national belonging and consciousness needed to mobilize citizens around a sense of common heritage and national identity.

Firstly, the image of a nation is usually represented in stories about the dominant ethnic group. In the context of English identity in the Euro 2012 tournament, despite England's changing multi-ethnic and racial base, it focused on the White English players and rather less on the eight men of color in the 23-man English squad.

Secondly, a shared sense of national belonging and consciousness is usually celebrated and reaffirmed through a common heritage and history. (Re)connecting citizens with that common heritage is done through national signifiers or symbols that evoke selective, emotive rituals, values, principles, and invented traditions. Hobsbawm defined invented traditions as:

> A set of practices, normally governed by overtly or tacitly accepted rules and of a ritual or symbolic nature, which seek to inculcate certain values and norms of behaviour by repetition, which automatically implies continuity with the past.[41]

Hobsbawm[42] noted that it was historians, politicians, and journalists that created the customs, myths, symbols, and rituals of national culture and that national identity was a selective idealized construction of a nation's historical and mythological accounts to produce a shared sense of national consciousness and identity.

Football championships provide an opportunity to view common public expressions of national identity. In the past, English supporters have shown their national pride through faces painted with the St. George cross, the wearing of replica and retro England shirts and through dressing in costumes signifying traditional Englishness such as Second World War era Royal Air Force pilot outfits and Crusaders from the Richard the Lionheart era. Hobsbawm noted that through such antics, 'The imagined community of millions seems more real as a team ... the individual, even the one who only cheers, becomes a symbol of the nation himself'.[43]

Thirdly, nations have common sets of civil rights and entitlements for their people, along with civic duties and responsibilities. Thus, as Tuck observed, English coaches and players become symbolic 'patriots at play', or 'embodiments of the nation' and are expected to be positive role models and ambassadors of the national culture.[44] This makes the deportment and behavior of English coaches and players subject to review and critique by journalists.

Fourthly, a nation's distinct identity is reflected through the creation of common enemies, usually as 'us vs. them' discourses. O'Donnell articulated how the format of international sport provides the ideal context for nations to '... act out their preferred myths through self-and other-stereotypes, and celebrate those qualities in which, ... in short make them superior'.[45]

Methodology

Textual analysis

We utilized textual analysis, an unobtrusive and non-reactive tool that reveals both subtle and explicit meanings in media content.[46] Specifically we analyzed how English national identity was (re)constructed through the selected newspapers narratives about the England team and their supporters during the Euro 2102 tournament. The two newspapers chosen for the analysis here have consistently ranked amongst the best-selling daily newspapers in England for some time. Moreover, these publications have been used in a range of research on media texts that have looked at the performances of England's national football team in major international tournaments over the years.[47,48,49,50] Analysis of narratives in the *Daily Mirror* and *The Sun* provides insight about English national identity through auto-typification of self-image, or how the nation talks to itself. Through our methodology we employed multiple levels of inductive coding merged with larger theoretical conceptualizations of national identity as a means of analysis. The specific texts, methods, and analysis are explained in Appendix 1.

Results

In total, 52 newspaper editions were analyzed. Ten themes emerged from the textual analysis:

'Land of no hope and glory'

In the months leading up to Euro 2012, the English team had been beset by problems. John Terry, the England team captain, was involved in an unsavory, heated verbal exchange with Queens Park Rangers' central defender, Anton Ferdinand, and was subsequently charged with racially abusing Ferdinand. In response, the Football Association (FA) relieved him of the English team captaincy without consulting the England manager, Fabio Capello. The Italian Capello, was incensed at this development and promptly resigned. Harry Redknapp, the media's preferred candidate for the position, and an Englishman widely considered the 'people's choice' for the job, was acquitted of tax evasion on the same day that Capello resigned. Despite the media clamor for Redknapp, the FA waited until almost the end of the EPL season to appoint another Englishman, Roy Hodgson, to the position. Appointed barely a month before the start of the Euro 2012 tournament, Hodgson had minimal preparation time. A further controversy erupted as Hodgson included John Terry in the England squad when some thought that Rio Ferdinand (Anton's brother) was a better choice. Further issues followed, including a rash of injuries and the loss of English talisman, Wayne Rooney, who was suspended for the first two games.

Set against this chain of events, the *Daily Mirror* and *The Sun's* build-up to Euro 2012 was remarkably subdued. Devoid of the usual hype and hope, columnist Andy Dunn lamented,

> Of a dozen writers and experts polled ... only one predicted England would advance beyond the quarter-finals ... Expectations have rarely been so low.

> In football terms, we have become the land of no hope and no glory. (*Daily Mirror*, 10 June 2012, p. 64)

The last sentence said it all. An inventive play of words on England's unofficial national anthem, 'Land of Hope and Glory', it epitomized Britain's loss of prestige since the days when it was composed by English composer Edward Elgar in 1902 at the height of the British Empire. Reflecting England's slim chances of winning the tournament, it also illustrated the crisis of identity as the country had fallen from its empire greatness. Undaunted, on the eve of England's first match, the *Daily Mirror* editorial expressed hope that '... unburdened by expectations' that the England team would '... cheer us all up' (*Daily Mirror*, 11 June 2012, p. 8).

'They think it's all Dover'

The first tenet of Guibernau's[51] strategies was to unite citizens around a collective national identity that featured the indigenous and dominant ethnic group. As such, these stories rarely reflected the full spectrum of ethnicities and races that comprised the national population. In this context, despite the multi-ethnic country England has become, this would reflect an emphasis on the predominantly White composition of the English team.

Both newspapers narratives drew on an outdated, White, homogenous, imagery of Englishness, anchored in the 'invented traditions' of the Second World War and the 1966 World Cup. Typical of this theme, under the inventive headline 'They think it's all Dover', *The Sun* featured a photograph of a giant 100 foot 'Roy the Redeemer' stature. Strategically, the image was placed on the white cliffs of Dover by bookmakers Paddy Power overlooking the English Channel, facing France. Adding to the effect, Hodgson's head was superimposed on a re-creation of the famous Christ the Redeemer statue in Rio de Janeiro '... in the hope of unsettling the French' (*The Sun*, 8 June 2012, p. 4). The headline 'They think it's all Dover' simultaneously evoked the popular World War Two song, '(There'll Be Bluebirds Over) The White Cliffs of Dover', made famous by Dame Vera Lynn in 1942, and Kenneth Wolstenholme's fourteen famous words as Geoff Hurst scored the final goal in 1966: 'Some people are on the pitch ... they think it's all over ... It is now!' This illustrated the creative puns and imaginative approaches found in the 'red-top' newspapers to capture the interest of the English 'imagined community'. It also reflected English playwright Alan Bennett's notion that English humor tends to contain equal measures of playfulness and seriousness. The image also evoked two bygone eras, the Second World War and the 1966 World Cup, both times when English national culture was more homogenous. It would ring few bells with the multiethnic minority that today constitute England's culturally diverse nation but would resonate well with the White majority who remember those days and prefer them to the multiethnic England of today.[52] In right-wing political imagery, the white cliffs of Dover are '... nation-defining ramparts', which symbolically serve to protect the nation from foreign '... contamination'.[53] Non-coincidentally, '(There'll Be Bluebirds Over) The White Cliffs of Dover' was recently coopted by the the British National Party for an anti-immigration album.

Symbols of ye olde England: 'men in George suits'

Guibernau's notion that a shared sense of national belonging and consciousness was usually (re)connected and celebrated through expressions of a common heritage and history was found in both newspapers' coverage of English supporters traveling to support the team in Poland and the Ukraine.[54] Numerous articles and photographs featured the English supporters' expressions of Englishness. The creation of dedicated fan zones (which debuted in the 2006 World Cup) provided the ideal space for English supporters to congregate and express their Englishness and support for the En-ger-land. Many were featured photographically wearing replica and retro England shirts with their faces and torsos painted in the Cross of Saint George. Others were pictured in a variety of costumes and regalia, such as Crusaders sporting chained mail and the Cross of St. George. Dubbed the 'men in George suits' (MIGS) by *The Sun*, all were playful parodies of traditional, idealized versions of the English identity. All the English supporters appeared to be enjoying the carnivalesque ambience and reveling in the 'performative community'.[55]

Both newspapers featured the same photograph of two MIGS posing with Swedish supporters in their yellow and blue national replica shirts, in a display of what Carrington described as '... shared public displays and mass mediated spectacles of nationhood'.[56] Nick Parker, the Chief Foreign Correspondent reporting from Kiev, commented,

> Amid a sea of Scandinavians in yellow and blue shirts, 'crusader' supporters Stan Stanfield and Dex Marshall epitomized the nation's bulldog spirit. The plucky pair braved playful jeers to stand on tables chanting 'Eng-er-land!' in an open-air bar packed with 1000 Swedes before posing for snaps with their rivals. (*The Sun*, 15 June 2012, pp. 4–5)

The image of middle-aged, White, Englishmen dressed in George suits exemplifying the 'bulldog spirit' epitomized 'ye olde England', the idealized England of yester-year. As Guibernau noted, '... antiquity acts as a source of legitimacy for the nation and the national identity associated with it'.[57] However, despite the appearance of good natured, almost self-deprecating parodies, the MIGS also reflected 'traces of faintly xenophobic self-satisfaction'.[58]

Gilroy articulated 'there ain't no black in the Union Jack'.[59] Twenty-five years later, notable by their almost complete absence were photographs of colored English supporters in either newspaper. One exception was as English minorities were pictured and quoted in response to former England player, Sol Campbell's, recommendations that colored English people not travel to Ukraine because of Ukraine's acknowledged problem with racism, a fact aired in the Panorama TV program that highlighted the prevalence of racism in Polish and Ukraine football clubs.

Lie back, Rio, and think of England

The exclusion of experienced central defender Rio Ferdinand, omitted from the squad in favor of John Terry, was to evoke more controversy, as Gary Cahill had to withdraw from the squad. Liverpool's inexperienced Martin Kelly, instead of Ferdinand, replaced him. Patronizingly, sport journalist Steven Howard suggested that because he is English 'Hodgson has been treated far more kindly than his predecessors' over the Ferdinand issue (*The Sun*, 8 June 2012, p. 73). Fuel was added to the controversy as on the same day in the *Daily Mirror*, Laurent Blanc, the manager of England's first opponent, France, was quoted saying 'I know Rio Ferdinand–he is a very good player–and I think that the choice to not take him isn't a sporting choice (p. 75). On the same day, in the same newspaper, former Scottish international player Kenny Dalglish, opined,

> Ferdinand is as good a central defender as there is. He is certainly as good as any English center-back. I feel for him if he is not going to the tournament for some reason other than football. (p. 79)

These comments, from a French manager and a former Scottish player, both considered antithetical to English interests, illustrate how contemporary sport journalists use quotes to personalize stories and create controversy in the build-up to a match.

Identified as 'quote culture',[60] these narratives are designed to inflame England's imagined community, and add to newspapers' marketing appeal.

On the same day, Rio Ferdinand was pictured relaxing on a sun lounger while on holiday in Cyprus, '... wearing red flowery shorts' under a headline, 'Lie back, Rio, and think of England' (*The Sun*, 8 June 2012, p. 8). In this way, *The Sun* framed Ferdinand in chauvinist terms normally reserved for women, featuring them as passive, subordinate, and sexually objectified.[61] Adding insult to injury, the characterization compounded the racist issue by feminizing Ferdinand.

Until England's defeat against Italy the specter of racism in both newspapers was directed at other nations, particularly joint host nation the Ukraine. Rod Liddle, a controversial print, radio, and television journalist, reported that Oleg Blokhin, Ukraine's manager, advised young Ukrainian footballer players to learn from fellow Ukrainians '... not from some zumba-bumba whom they took out of a tree gave two bananas and now ... plays in the Ukrainian league' (*The Sun*, 21 June 2012, p.13). Liddle noted that the English side that had just beaten Ukraine contained a number of colored players, which made it 'a double pleasure to see his (Blokhin's) side booted out the tournament'. Liddle concluded: 'Zumba-bumbas 1, Oleg Blockhead 0' (*The Sun*, 21 June 2012, p.13). Both newspapers' narratives glossed over England's own racial issues until their elimination by Italy on penalties. During the shoot-out, Ashley Cole and Ashley Young, both colored, failed to convert their penalties. Both newspapers reported how both players were abused by 'racist trolls' on social media platform Twitter.

'Death camp visit'

Nations usually formalize a common set of civil rights and entitlements for their citizens, along with concomitant civic duties, expectations, and responsibilities. These expectations include 'good citizen' qualities in the Guibernau's national identity matrix.[62] During Euro 2012, it was the English coaches and players that became highly visible symbolic 'patriots at play', and 'embodiments of the nation'.[63] Thus, they were expected to be positive role models and ambassadors of the national character and culture. This made the coaches' and players' behavior and deportment subject to scrutiny by the journalists for their 'imagined community'. Epitomizing this type of narrative was the visit to the Nazi extermination camps at Auschwitz and Birkenau by Hodgson and seven of the English players. Under the headline 'Death Camp Visit', seven English players were pictured walking under the infamous 'Arbeit Macht Frei, (work sets you free) sign. Oliver Holt reported the English players' visit made a '... powerful statement'. Former Chelsea manager, Avram Grant, who lost relatives in the Holocaust, was quoted:

> It was so important they came. People will see them here and then more people will come. It is important that people do not forget what happened here and the England players have great power to spread that message. (*Daily Mirror*, 9 June 2012, pp. 6–7)

'Long to Wayne over us'

Despite the contemporary trends of globalization and transnationalism, Gilroy noted how the nation state and national identity has been strengthened through a 'new priority attached to security'.[64] In the aftermath of homegrown terrorism experienced in London on 7/7, there were renewed calls for immigrants to fully integrate into

British society and culture. As part of this, a British history and culture exam was introduced as a component of the British citizenship program. Additionally, applicants were required to perform an oath of allegiance to the Queen and learn the words of the national anthem, 'God Save the Queen.' Before all international games, both teams' national anthems are always sung. As 'representatives of the nation', the English players became scrutinized to see if they sang the anthem with gusto or paid little attention to it. Under the headline 'Long to Wayne over us', (a reworking of the line 'Long to reign over us') foreign correspondents Charlie Wyett and Nick Parker reported how England manager Roy Hodgson '… ordered his players '… to belt out 'God Save the Queen' to demonstrate their pride in representing the country and proudly flying its flag' (*The Sun*, 22 June 2012, pp. 6–7). No mention was made about the anachronism of using the British national anthem. Instead Hodgson's directive was viewed very favorably in the narratives. Piers Morgan, a former editor of the *Daily Mirror* was reported to have tweeted, 'At last … Wayne Rooney sings the National Anthem. Good lad, Shrek' (*Daily Mirror*, 21 June 2012, p. 7). Again, it was a perfect example of the 'accustomed exaggeration' and caricature style found in the 'red-top' newspapers for the entertainment of their readers.[65]

'Courage, fortitude, discipline'

As 'embodiments of the nation', English football players were expected to live up to quintessential English characteristics and qualities. These characteristics emerged during the age of imperialism when the British/English code of civility was revered for its socializing influence on colonial subjects.[66] Since that time, the code has permeated through all levels of British society, including sport. Back in 1966, Weight noted how England's manager, Alf Ramsey, personified 'emotional reserve' and '… believed in the stiff upper lip of the English gentleman'.[67] Ramsey's players were personified as being resolute, resilient, and lion-hearted. Since then these characteristics have been passed on as the standards that all English players must meet.

Forty-six years later, the England team was again managed by an Englishman, Roy Hodgson. Depicted as being 'cut from the same cloth' as Ramsey and other successful English managers (such as Terry Venables and Bobby Robson) and in sharp contrast to his predecessor, Fabio Capello, Hodgson was praised for '… knowing how to get the best out of his fellow countrymen' (*Daily Mirror*, 23 June 2012, p. 67). England's new manager was also credited with instilling '… courage, fortitude, and discipline' in a group of English players who played '… for their manager, themselves, and the shirt' (*Daily Mirror*, 21 June 2012, pp. 70–71). After finishing top of their group, the English team received plaudits for their new national spirit and displays of traditional English effort. All were attributed to Hodgson's leadership along with their '… defensive defiance and resilience', both considered 'hallmarks of Hodgson teams' (*Daily Mirror*, 21 June 2012, p. 70). Individually, the players' English qualities were highlighted in media narratives. Goalkeeper Joe Hart was described as having '… RAF stiff upper lip written all over him' (*The Sun*, 8 June 2012, p. 74). Scott Parker, in his defensive, holding midfielder role, was described as '… the epitome of … selflessness', and praised for his willingness to make sacrifices for the greater good' (*Daily Mirror*, 23 June 2012, pp. 70–71).

England's elimination in a penalty shootout against Italy in the semifinal did not halt the outpouring of national support for Hodgson's team. Instead of the usual maudlin inquest on England's failure to win the trophy, most journalists praised the

English effort. Typifying this was the *Daily Mirror's* headline that read, 'A triumph of pride and courage … England fought on long after it was clear they were playing a superior side' (*Daily Mirror*, 25 June 20,102, pp. 60–61). Martin Lipton, chief football writer, lamented, 'While Roy Hodgson has changed so much about this squad, while they were, indeed, 'bulldogs', in the end it counted for nothing' (*Daily Mirror*, 25 June 2012, pp. 62–63).

'Us vs. them'

Guibernau's national identity typology[68] suggests that countries mobilize national cohesiveness among their citizens by promoting negative narratives and images about 'foreigners.' These discourses reinforce the national sense of 'who we are' by contrasting 'us' from the undesirable characteristics of 'them'. Aughey noted that 'red-top' newspapers employ narratives that 'only the politically tone deaf could fail to hear … because there are equal measures of playfulness and seriousness', a style that '… is a living icon of modern Englishness' (p. 197). This can be achieved subtly through nuanced and progressive narratives (the non-Red-Top approach) or it can be done by bludgeoning the readership with exaggerated insular, parochial, 'little Englander' 'us vs. them' ideologies. The *Daily Mirror* and *The Sun's* adopted the latter approach.

'Let's give 'em a new Waterloo'

Before England played France in its opening group match, both newspapers framed France as '… one of England's old enemies, along with Scotland and Germany' (*Sunday Mirror*, 10 June 2012, p. 14). Reaching back in time, the *Daily Mirror* editorial drew on an 'us vs. them' rhetoric, evoking the 'invented tradition' of the battle of Waterloo thus:

> It certainly isn't impossible that tomorrow the French will leave the field whipped, their Gallic tails between their legs. That wouldn't just be the best result over them since Bryan Robson scored twice in the 1982 clash, but the most sensational since we crushed them at Waterloo in 1815. And this time they haven't got Napoleon leading the attack. (10 June 2012, p. 14)

The following day under the headline 'Raider of the Crossed Arc' (an inventive re-working of the popular movie title Raiders of the Lost Ark), *The Sun* featured a photograph of the Arc de Triomphe and the Eiffel tower with a giant Saint George Cross flag superimposed on them. Journalist Emily Nash reported:

> England aim to get one over on the French today – just like we did by beaming a giant St George's Cross on to the Arc de Triomphe. *The Sun* caught the French defence napping with our display of patriotism – and hopefully Roy Hodgson and his men can follow suit. (*The Sun*, 11 June 2012, pp. 4–5)

The 'us vs. them' invective continued in the sports section. Under the headline 'Cap'n Steve fired up by French jibes', sports journalist Steven Howard reported how 'ANGLO-FRENCH hostilities' broke out during the pre-game press conference when '… a mickey-taking' French journalist asked Steven Gerrard, the English team Captain, if England could still be considered '… a serious footballing nation when they have not won a tournament since 1966' (*The Sun*, 11 June 2012, pp. 58–59). Incensed, Gerrard reacted as though:

He … wasn't going to stand for foreigners putting the knife in especially that lot over the other side of the channel.

He metaphorically,

> … followed the historic example of the English archers at Agincourt who flicked a communal V-sign at their French counterparts on the famous day in 1415. (*The Sun*, 11 June 2012, pp. 58–59)

The English supporters who watched England eke out a 1–1 draw in a dull game were reported as having followed their captain's defiant lead in the press conference. They entertained each other and surrounding crowds by renditions of patriotic songs such as 'England 'Til I Die' and the theme from the 'Great Escape'. Oliver Harvey reported the English supporters' less than '… sophisticated' commentary about 'Anglo-French relations' in their cheeky rendition of 'you can stick your f****** Euro up your a***', sung to the tune of 'She'll Be Coming Round the Mountain'. (*The Sun*, 12 June 2012, p. 6–7)

'Och aye the Roo'

Both newspapers reported in an 'us vs. them' format how well the English players had responded to the ultra-patriotic overtures of their fellow Englishmen. Roy Hodgson's English man-management style was contrasted with the austere, strict, disciplinarian approach of former Italian manager, Fabio Capello. Capello was widely derided in the popular English press for suggesting he only needed to know 100 English words to manage the England team. His inability to master the English language was deliberately exposed and played upon by journalists during press conferences in his time as England manager. In the build-up to England's quarterfinal match against Italy, Wayne Rooney was quoted as saying that the English players were pleased that under Hodgson 'nothing is lost in translation' (*The Sun*, 21 June 2012, p. 5). After England's defeat to Italy (which featured a sub-par Rooney performance) under the inventive headline 'Och Aye the Roo', sports reporter Martin Lipton reported how Capello '… put the boot into Wayne Rooney, blaming him for England's EURO 2012 exit' (*Daily Mirror*, 27 June 2012, front page of sports section). Further, Capello was quoted saying:

> After watching the last game (England's lost to Italy) I think that Rooney understands only Scottish. That's because he only plays well in Manchester, where Sir Alex Ferguson speaks Scottish. (Daily Mirror, 27 June 2012, p. 63)

Through this tongue-in-cheek comment, Capello showed that while his command of English was not perfect, he well understood the English mentality and the traditional enmity that exists between Scotland and England. He understood that the majority of Scottish football supporters will support 'anyone but England'.[69] Capello had learned a few things during his four-year tenure at the England managerial helm.

Concluding remarks

This study provides a snapshot of how English identity was portrayed through the English national football team and their supporters during Euro 2012 in selected 'red-top' English newspapers. It illustrates how media narratives, however obtuse, nuanced, or bombastic, conform to generalized guidelines such as Guibernau's[70] framework to generate a sense of national unity and consciousness. They illustrate how often media relies on national heritage, history, and culture for their imagery in drawing audiences towards what Maguire termed 'wilful nostalgia', a yearning to return to a mythical golden age when their country was 'great'.[71] Certainly the approach works for the English media. Whether it works for countries with less-storied heritages remains to be seen.

Paul McCarthy, an English sport media consultant and a former sports journalist, noted how much sport journalists rely on the '... tried and tested formula' of old concepts and ideas, warmed over and revamped, in contemporary reporting.[72] This proved to be the case during Euro 2012 as old ideas were reintroduced in almost for-mulaic fashion depicting (in the English case) 'our finest hour' during the Second World War; 'the boys of summer in '66'; the 'us vs. them' rhetoric, and the constant referrals back to mythical, bygone eras.

But such findings are useful in emphasizing what factors have retained their importance in the formation of national cultures. In the English case, it shows how central and ingrained Second World War folklore remains in English national iden-tity. In England's footballing world, it demonstrates the importance of the 1966 World Cup win in the footballing psyche of the country that invented the modern game. It also shows the national hurt that occurs every time the national team falls short of the country's expectations. But hope springs eternal. Nevermind the reality that experts believed England had little chance of repeating the success of 'the boy's of '66' anytime soon. But with each passing competition, England's status as a sec-ond-tier football power inches a little closer towards the eventual realization that the world has changed, and with it, football. Culturally and emotionally, Britain, let alone England, has barely got past its empire glory days. There has not yet been general acceptance, in football or globally, of the country's general decline or as Gilroy termed it, 'postcolonial melancholia'.[73]

Culturally, despite England's colonial experiences and its key involvement in two world wars, the country has never graduated to the global maturity that other, more involved countries in Europe have done. Britain was created as an island. Geographically and psychically separated from the rest of Europe, it has remained a law unto itself. We see this in our analysis of England as it clings to its outdated notions of the dominant ethnic group and its repeated failure to acknowledge the realities of the new multi-ethnic England. This will undoubtedly change, but only over time as colored players slowly change the minds of their 'army' of supporters who still see themselves in the media's eyes as representatives of 'ye olde England.' The English, like all nations, will accept the inevitable, but only after they have pursued all other options. They learn bit by bit, and their realization comes only slowly. In this, the media play a crucial role. Publicity over racism and the John Terry incident, when added to similar occurrences, will eventually draw the appropriate universal condemnation. Similarly, the 'us vs. them' rhetoric, no matter how adroitly and subtly crafted, may fade as history does in the national psyche.

But in the meantime, journalists will continue to work with what they have. The fact remains that Britain, created out of the Atlantic Ocean over 2½ billion years ago, remains separated from the rest of Europe and the world. This geographic sepa-ration has led to a psychic distancing of the English and/or British from everyone else. This is reflected in its journalism and its sports. Its sports have been generally acknowledged as contributing to world peace and understanding. Its journalism sustains its national energies as a people. That the two are at odds with each other … is perhaps immaterial.

Notes

1. Montserrat Guibernau, *The Identity of Nations* (Cambridge: Polity, 2007).
2. Guibernau, *The Identity of Nations*, 11.
3. Bhiku Parekh, 'Discourses on National Identity', *Political Studies*, 42 (1994): 5.
4. Benedict R. Anderson, *Imagined Communities: Reflections on the Origin and the Spread of Nationalism* (London: Verso, 1983).
5. Eric J. Hobsbawm, *Nations and Nationalism since 1780* (Cambridge: Cambridge University Press, 1990).
6. Stuart Hall, 'Old and New Identities, Old and New Ethnicities', In *Culture, Globalization and the World-System*, ed. A. King (London: Macmillan, 1991), 57.
7. Anthony D. Smith, *National Identity* (Harmondsworth: Penguin).
8. Guibernau, *The Identity of Nations*, 169.
9. Hobsbawm, *Nations and Nationalism since 1780*, 143.
10. Richard Giulianotti, *Football: A Sociology of the Game* (Cambridge: Polity Press, 1999), 4.
11. Gerd von der Lippe, 'Media Image: Sport, Gender and National Identities in Five European Countries', *Internaional Review for the Sociology of Sport*, 37 (2002): 374.
12. David Rowe et al., 'Come Together: Sport, Nationalism, and the Media Image', in *MediaSport*, ed. L.A. Wenner (London: Routledge, 1998), 133.
13. Garry Whannel, *Culture, Politics and Sport: Blowing the Whistle, Revisted* (London: Routledge, 2008).
14. John S. Hunter, 'Flying the Flag: Identities, the Nation, and Sport', *Identities: Global Studies in Culture and Power*, 10 (2003).
15. John Vincent and John S. Hill, 'Flying the Flag for the En-ger-land: The Sun's (Re)presentation of English Identity During the 2010 World Cup', *Journal of Sport & Tourism*, 6 (2011).
16. Richard Weight, *Patriots. National Identity in Britain 1940–2000* (Basingstoke: Macmillan, 2002).
17. Weight, *Patriots*, 461.
18. Ibid., *Patriots*, 459.
19. John Harris and Ben Clayton, 'David Beckham and the Changing (Re)presentations of English Identity', *International Journal of Sport Management and Marketing*, 2 (2007).
20. Vincent and Hill, 'Flying the Flag'.
21. Joseph Maguire and Emma K. Poulton, 'European Identity Politics in Euro 96: Invented Traditions and National Habitus Codes', *International Review for the Sociology of Sport*, 34 (1999).
22. Joseph Maguire et al., 'Weltkrieg III? Media Coverage of England vs. Germany in Euro 96', *Journal of Sport & Social Issues*, 23 (1999a).
23. Joseph Maguire et al., 'The War of Words? Identity Politics in Anglo-German Press Coverage of Euro 96', *European Journal of Communication*, 14 (1999b).
24. John Vincent et al., 'England Expects: English Newspapers' Narratives about the English Football Team in the 2006 World Cup', *International Review for the Sociology of Sport*, 45 (2010).
25. See also Harris and Clayton, 'David Beckham'.
26. Krishan Kumar, *The Making of English National Identity* (Cambridge: Cambridge University Press, 2003).
27. Krishan Kumar, 'English and British National Identity', *History Compass*, 4 (2006).
28. Robert Colls, 'Review of "The Making of English Identity"', *The Sociological Review*, 53 (2005).
29. John G.A. Pocock, 'Gaberlunzie's Return', *New Left Review* (second series), 5 (2000).
30. Arthur Aughey, *The Politics of Englishness* (Manchester: Manchester University, 2007).
31. Kumar, *The Making of English National Identity*.

32. Tom Nairn, *Faces of Nationalism: Janus Revisited* (London: Verso, 1977).
33. Ben Wellings, 'Empire-Nation: National and Imperial Discourses in England', *Nations & Nationalism*, 8 (2002).
34. David Gervais, 'Englands of the Mind', *The Cambridge Quarterly*, 30 (2001).
35. Nairn, *Faces of Nationalism*.
36. Raphaël Ingelbein, *Misreading England: Poetry and Nationhood since the Second World War* (Amsterdam: Rodopi, 2002).
37. Weight, *Patriots*, 450.
38. Aughey, *The Politics of Englishess*.
39. Eric Hobsbawm, 'Introduction: Inventing Traditions', in *The Invention of Tradition*, ed. E.J. Hobsbawm and T.O. Ranger (Cambridge: Cambridge University Press, 1983).
40. Guibernau, *The Identity of Nations*, 25.
41. Hobsbawm, 'Introduction: Inventing Traditions', 1.
42. Hobsbawm, *Nations and Nationalism*.
43. Hobsbawm, *Nations and Nationalism*, 1473.
44. Jason Tuck, 'The Men in White: Reflections on Rugby Union, the Media and Englishness', *International Review for the Sociology of Sport*, 38 (2003).
45. Hugh O'Donnell, 'Mapping the Mythical: A Geopolitics of National Sporting Stereotypes', *Discourse and Society*, 5 (1994): 353.
46. Alan McKee, 'A Beginner's Guide to Textual Analysis', *Metro* (*Film, Television, Radio, Multimedia*), 127 (2003).
47. John Harris, 'Lie Back and Think of England: The Women of Euro "96"', *Journal of Sport and Social Issues*, 23 (1999).
48. Harris and Clayton, 'David Beckham'.
49. Vincent and Hill, 'Flying the Flag'.
50. Vincent et al., 'England Expects'.
51. Guibernau, *The Identity of Nations*.
52. Roger Scruton, *The Need for Nations* (London: Civitas, 2004).
53. Paul Gilroy, *Postcolonial Melancholia* (New York: Columbia University Press, 2005), 14.
54. Guibernau, *The Identity of Nations*.
55. Tim Crabbe, 'Postmodern Community and Future Directions. Fishing for Community: England Fans at the 2006 FIFA World Cup', *Soccer & Society*, 9 (2008): 435.
56. Ben Carrington, 'Too many St. George Crosses to Bear', in *The Ingerland Factor: Home Truths from Football*, ed. M. Perryman (London: Mainstream, 1999), 72.
57. Guibernau, *The Identity of Nations*, 173.
58. Tim Crabbe, 'endlandfans – A New Club for a New England? Social Inclusion, Authenticity and the Performance of Englishness at "Home" and "Away"', *Leisure Studies*, 23 (2004): 72.
59. Paul Gilroy, *There Ain't no Black in the Union Jack: The Cultural Politics of Race and Nation* (London: Hutchinson, 1987).
60. Raymond Boyle, *Sports Journalism: Context and Issues* (London: Sage, 2006), 42.
61. See Harris, 'Lie Back and Think of England'.
62. Guibernau, *The Identity of Nations*.
63. See Tuck, 'The Men in White'.
64. Gilroy, *Postcolonial Melancholia*, 59.
65. Aughey, *The Politics of Englishness*.
66. Kumar, 'English and British National Identity'.
67. Weight, *Patriots*, 458.
68. Guibernau, *The Identity of Nations*.
69. Alan Bairner, *Sport, Nationalism and Globalization: European and North American Perspectives* (Albany: SUNY Press, 2001), 51.
70. Guibernau, *The Identity of Nations*.
71. Joseph Maguire, *Global Sport: Identities, Societies, Civilizations* (Cambridge: Polity, 1999), 191.
72. Paul McCarthy, 'Newspaper Review', *Sky Sports News*, BSkyB, November 21, 2012.
73. Gilroy, *Postcolonial Melancholia*.
74. John W. Creswell, *Research Design: Qualitative, Quantitative, and Mixed Methods Approaches* 2nd ed. (Thousand Oaks, CA: Sage, 2003).

75. Anselm Strauss and Juliet Corbin, *Basics of Qualitative Research: Grounded Theory Procedures and Techniques* 2nd ed. (Newbury Park, CA: Sage, 1999).
76. William Lawrence Neuman, *The Meanings of Methodology: Social Research Methods* 5th ed. (Boston, MA: Allyn & Bacon, 2003), 443.
77. Strauss and Corbin, *Basics of Qualitative Research*.
78. Catherine Marshall and Gretchen B. Rossman, *Designing Qualitative Research* 4th ed. (Thousand Oaks, CA: Sage, 2006).
79. Norman Fairclough, *Analysing Discourse: Textual Analysis for Social Research* (London: Routledge, 2003), 16.

References

Anderson, Benedict R. *Imagined Communities Reflections on the Origin and the Spread of Nationalism*. London: Verso, 1983.

Aughey, Arthur. *The Politics of Englishness*. Manchester: Manchester University Press, 2007.

Bairner, Alan. *Sport, Nationalism and Globalization: European and North American Perspectives*. Albany: SUNY Press, 2001.

Boyle, Raymond. *Sports Journalism: Context and Issues*. London: Sage, 2006.

Carrington, Ben. 'Too Many St. George Crosses to Bear'. In *The Ingerland Factor: Home Truths from Football*, ed. M. Perryman, 71–86. London: Mainstream, 1999.

Colls, Robert. 'Review of 'The Making of English Identity'. *The Sociological Review* 53 (2005): 581–3.

Crabbe, Tim. 'englandfans – A New Club for a New England? Social Inclusion, Authenticity and the Performance of Englishness at 'Home' and 'Away''. *Leisure Studies* 23 (2004): 63–78.

Crabbe, Tim. 'Postmodern Community and Future Directions. Fishing for Community: England Fans at the 2006 FIFA World Cup'. *Soccer & Society* 9 (2008): 428–38.

Creswell, John W. *Research Design Qualitative, Quantitative, and Mixed Methods Approaches*. 2nd ed. Thousand Oaks, CA: Sage, 2003.

Fairclough, Norman. *Analysing Discourse: Textual Analysis for Social Research*. London: Routledge, 2003.

Gervais, David. 'Englands of the Mind'. *The Cambridge Quarterly* 30 (2001): 151–68.

Gilroy, Paul. *There Ain't no Black in the Union Jack: The Cultural Politics of Race and Nation*. London: Hutchinson, 1987.

Gilroy, Paul. *Postcolonial Melancholia*. New York: Columbia University Press, 2005.

Giulianotti, Richard. *Football: A sociology of the game*. Cambridge: Polity Press, 1999.

Guibernau, Montserrat. *The Identity of Nations*, Cambridge: Polity, 2007.

Hall, Stuart. 'Old and New Identities, Old and New Ethnicities'. In *Culture, Globalization and the World-System*, ed. A. King, 41–68. London: Macmillan, 1991.

Harris, John. 'Lie Back and Think of England: The Women of Euro '96''. *Journal of Sport and Social Issues* 23 (1999): 96–110.

Harris, John, and Ben Clayton. 'David Beckham and the Changing (Re)presentations of English Identity'. *International Journal of Sport Management and Marketing* 2 (2007): 208–21.

Hobsbawm, Eric. 'Introduction: Inventing Traditions'. In *The Invention of Tradition*, ed. E.J. Hobsbawn and T.O. Ranger, 1–14. Cambridge: Cambridge University Press, 1983.

Hobsbawm, Eric J. *Nations and Nationalism Since 1780*. Cambridge: Cambridge University Press, 1990.

Hunter, John S. 'Flying the Flag: Identities, the Nation, and Sport'. *Identities: Global Studies in Culture and Power* 10 (2003): 409–25.

Ingelbien, Raphaël. *Misreading England: Poetry and Nationhood since the Second World War*. Amsterdam: Rodopi, 2002.

Kumar, Krishan. *The Making of English National Identity*. Cambridge: Cambridge University Press, 2003.

Kumar, Krishan. 'English and British National Identity'. *History Compass* 4 (2006): 428–47.

Maguire, Joseph. *Global Sport: Identities, Societies, Civilizations*. Cambridge: Polity, 1999.

Maguire, Joseph, and Emma K. Poulton. 'European Identity Politics in Euro 96: Invented Traditions and National Habitus Codes'. *International Review for the Sociology of Sport* 34 (1999): 17–29.

Maguire, J., Emma, Poulton, and Catherine Possamai. 'Weltkrieg III? Media coverage of England versus Germany in Euro 96'. *Journal of Sport & Social Issues* 23 (1999a): 439–54.

Maguire, J., Emma Poulton, and Catherine Possamai. 'The War of Words? Identity Politics in Anglo-German Press Coverage of Euro 96'. *European Journal of Communication* 14 (1999b): 61–89.

Marshall, Catherine, and Gretchen B. Rossman. *Designing Qualitative Research*. 4th ed. Thousand Oaks, CA: Sage, 2006.

McCarthy, Paul. 'Newspaper Review'. *Sky Sports News*, BSkyB, November 21, 2012.

McKee, Alan. 'A Beginner's Guide to Textual Analysis'. *Metro (Film Television Radio Multimedia)* 127 (2003): 138–49.

Nairn, Tom. *Faces of Nationalism: Janus Revisisted*. London: Verso, 1977.

Neuman, William Lawrence. *The Meanings of Methodology: Social Research Methods*. 5th ed. Boston, MA: Allyn & Bacon, 2003.

O'Donnell, Hugh. 'Mapping the Mythical: A Geopolitics of National Sporting Stereotypes'. *Discourse Society* 5 (1994): 345–80.

Parekh, Bhiku. 'Discourses on National Identity'. *Political Studies* 42 (1994): 492–504.

Pocock, John G.A. 'Gaberlunize's Return'. *New Left Review* (second series) 5 (2000): 41–52.

Rowe, David, Jim McKay, and Toby Miller. 'Come Together: Sport, Nationalism, and the Media Image'. In *MediaSport*, ed. L.A. Wenner, 119–33. London: Routledge, 1998.

Scruton, Roger. *The Need for Nations*. London: Civitas, 2004.

Smith, Anthony D. *National Identity*. Harmondsworth: Penguin, 1991.

Strauss, Anselm, and Juliet Corbin. *Basics of Qualitative Research: Grounded Theory Procedures and Technique*. 2nd ed. Newbury Park, CA: Sage, 1999.

Tuck, Jason. 'The Men in White: Reflections on Rugby Union, the Media and Englishness'. *International Review for the Sociology of Sport* 38 (2003): 177–99.

Vincent, John, Edward M. Kian, Paul M. Pedersen, Aaron Kuntz, and John S. Hill. 'Narratives about the English Football Team in the 2006 World Cup'. *International Review for the Sociology of Sport* 45 (2010): 199–223.

Vincent, John, and John S. Hill. 'Flying the Flag for the En-ger-land: The Sun's (Re)presentation of English Identity During the 2010 World Cup'. *Journal of Sport & Tourism* 6 (2011): 187–209.

von der Lippe, Gerd. 'Media Image: Sport, Gender and National Identities in Five European Countries'. *International Review for the Sociology of Sport* 37 (2002): 371–96.

Weight Richard. *Patriots. National Identity in Britain 1940–2000*. Basingstoke: Macmillan, 2002.

Wellings, Ben. 'Empire-Nation: National and Imperial Discourses in England'. *Nations & Nationalism* 8 (2002): 95–109.

Whannel, Garry. *Culture, Politics and Sport: Blowing the Whistle, Revisited*. London: Routledge, 2008.

Appendix 1. Detailed methods

The newspapers

We examined all articles on or related to Euro 2012 published in the hard copies of the *Daily Mirror* and *The Sun*, as well as their respective Sunday editions. These newspapers were chosen because of their national prominence and popularity and their extensive sports coverage. Data collection was from 7 June to 2 July 2012, which included the day prior to and the day after the tournament.

Coding procedures

As a means for generating multiple and layered elements of analyses, two specific levels of coding, *open* and *axial*, were used as part of our textual analysis of the newspaper articles. The resulting codes were then interpreted in relation to specific theoretical frameworks devoted to national identity. As a result, articles were coded inductively, yet interpreted through larger-ordered conceptualizations.

In order to achieve this, each article was read twice and narratives that were perceived to relate to aspects of English national identity in relation to the men's football team were highlighted with a marker pen before being typed into a Word document, arranged by newspaper and date. Included in the analysis were all articles about the English men's football team, on and off the field, as well as any commentaries about English supporters and discourses about national identity politics in the context of Euro 2012. At this stage, the Word document transcripts were examined multiple times with the goal of identifying dominant narratives as well as contradictions and inconsistencies. This form of open or thematic coding is an inductive analysis technique and as such employed a constant comparison method to search for, analyze, and interpret emerging themes.[74,75]

To begin, *open coding* was employed as an initial means of organizing raw document data into overarching themes and condensing the large amounts of data generated throughout the study. As Neuman noted, open coding brings themes to the surface from deep inside the data. The themes are at a low level of abstraction and come from the researcher's initial research focus, concepts in the literature, or new thoughts stimulated by immersion in the data.[76] Hand-in-hand with open coding, we also organized the data through *axial coding* as a means of linking previously identified themes and categories within the data. Axial coding links and relates codes to each other and brings greater depth to initial thematic codes.[77] Through axial coding, organizing themes developed which, in turn, were interpreted within the larger frameworks of national identity.

Analysis

The preliminary codes generated from this inductive process were then interpreted. This textual analysis does not aim to reproduce the newspapers' coverage or reporters' narratives, but to uncover the dominant or preferred readings about the national identity of the men's English team in the context of the Euro 2012.

Validity/Trustworthiness

Employing a methodology drawing upon multiple levels of coding and interpreting our data according to well-developed theoretical frameworks resulted in a reliable research design with validated analyses.[78] Our analytical methods were designed to ensure consistent data collection and analysis, thus providing more validity to our findings.

Limitations

While our coding process and data analysis offered insight into themes of national identity, it is important to recognize that like all theoretical interpretations of social constructs ours is not without its own set of limitations. As Fairclough noted, 'we cannot assume that a text in its full actuality can be made transparent through applying the categories of a pre-existing analytical framework'.[79] Thus, we acknowledge that our use of existing theories to organize and orient our analysis potentially excludes alternative interpretations of our data. Further, our use of close textual analysis sought to explicate the development of English national identity on both local and global levels, managing these overlapping discourses through multiple levels of coding. As such, our analytical strategies assumed that close readings of public documents, such as newspapers, reveal larger cultural sensibilities and systems of meaning-making.

German football culture in the new millennium: ethnic diversity, flair and youth on and off the pitch

Udo Merkel

School of Sport and Service Management, University of Brighton, Eastbourne, UK

Germany sent its most ethnically diverse team ever to Poland and Ukraine to compete in Euro 2012. Over the last six years, the Germany manager, Joachim Löw, has not only revitalized and rejuvenated his squad but also included a considerable number of players with foreign roots and from ethnic minorities. This ethnic and cultural diversity of the current German national side is the result of some major policy changes in the country at the turn of the millennium that made it easier for immigrants and their offspring to gain citizenship. In comparison with other European nations, it is not a reflection of a colonial history but a model of contemporary German society. This paper argues that the above-mentioned changes on the pitch are also reflected off it. Both the 2006 and 2010 Soccer World Cups and Euro 2012 turned into widespread and colourful celebrations of a new, modern sense of Germanness underpinned by a non-threatening and playful patriotism. The creativity, diversity, youth, style and flair of both the German team and its supporters presented the country as a confident and more embracing place than ever before.

Soccer and society: guarding and gaining collective identities

Modern football originated in England and arrived in Germany in the last quarter of the nineteenth century. The game was initially met with indifference, which rapidly turned into open hostility. Influential members of the national gymnastics movement, the *Turnbewegung*, tried to halt the spread of soccer. They labelled it the 'English Disease' and argued that this team sport was un-German, trivial, lacking a metaphysical underpinning and, therefore, decadent.[1] It was primarily the older and more conservative sections of the German middle class, the *Bürgertum*, that had initiated and orchestrated this resistance as they saw sports, such as football, as a threat to their own, distinctively different form of physical exercise, gymnastics (*Turnen*). Soccer as a representative of the new and modern concept of sport, they insisted, was a reflection of Western 'Zivilization' but did not belong to German 'Kultur'.[2] Furthermore,

> while modern sports contributed to the English middle class's attempts at class formation, they could hardly serve this function for the German *Bürgertum*. With regard to the latter's identity, sports played at most an ambivalent, but mainly a disintegrating role.[3]

In a nutshell, the introduction of football in Germany was accompanied by some intense debates about the country's collective identity, in particular the notion of Germanness.

However, the final decades of the nineteenth century witnessed a number of far-reaching socio-economic and lifestyle changes. Orthodox gymnastics did not seem to satisfy the physical and mental demands of the people any longer. 'The new generation wanted fresh air and play ... a natural reaction to new conditions of life',[4] which were caused by the rapid urbanization process, the expansion of industrial production and the growing fragmentation of everyday life. These modern quests for diversion, excitement and outdoor physical activities were met by team games, such as soccer. However, the first to take up and play this team sport on a fairly regular basis as part of their extracurricular activities in schools were the sons of the German middle class. Later, also a small number of male middle class adults took up this sport. The latter founded the first clubs, which quickly attracted members of the working class. This happened in towns like Braunschweig, Hamburg, Berlin, Leipzig, Karlsruhe and Nuremburg.[5]

Until the outbreak of World War I in 1914, playing football in Germany remained primarily 'a middle class affair'.[6] However, 'football's breakthrough in Germany was, by and large, less a result of private middle class initiative'[7] but driven by workers' sports clubs and associations. From the 1920s onwards, it became the sport of the German industrial working class, particularly in the Ruhr area, also known as the Ruhr valley, a heavily industrialized and densely populated region in North Rhine Westphalia. It remains a dominant geographical stronghold of the game and hosts internationally renowned clubs such as Borussia Dortmund and Schalke F.C. After the successful fight for the 8 h working day, in 1919, the foundation of working class soccer clubs accelerated in the early 1920s.

Membership in these organizations offered a sense of belonging and a distinctive identity, usually expressed through the name of the club, the choice of a distinctive colour combination, the flags, the banners, the pennants and a particular song. All these props represented the local community. Social interaction and cohesion was further promoted through practicing and playing together, participating in excursions and celebrations.[8] The predominantly working class inhabitants of the Ruhr valley faced two dilemmas: the speed and magnitude of social change and the lack of a common cultural history. Due to the emergence and expansion of industrial production in the Ruhr area at the turn of the twentieth century, there was a huge demand for additional workers. These were recruited from all over central Europe. Many of them came from areas that had once belonged to Prussia.

> While in 1861, there were altogether 16 (!) Polish living in the counties of Rhineland and Westphalia, in 1910, this number had increased to more than 30,000 ... Already in 1907, in many coalmines, the proportion of workers from the old German eastern areas and from Poland was higher than 50%.[9]

These migrant communities lacked common cultural roots and traditions. However, football clubs offered a flexible framework to develop and perform cultural practices. These were often borrowed from customs and traditions of the rural communities, from which these migrants originated. 'Most of the immigrants had come from rural areas and felt lost within the industrial setting of huge companies and the railways, not to speak of their own linguistic problems in a German-dominated environment'.[10] Putting it in Toennies' terms, one is tempted to suggest that due to the emergence of 'Gesellschaft', an increasingly complex and differentiated German society, those people affected kept up 'Gemeinschaft'-like patterns of life in certain enclaves. This enabled them to locate and identify their place in society. For these people, the active involvement in football clubs became an experience of particular socio-cultural depth and emotional intensity.

One century, three successful World Cup campaigns (1954, 1974 and 1990)[11] and three European Championships titles (1972, 1980 and 1996) later, the genuine and intense, economic, social and cultural bonds between clubs, teams and local communities have largely disappeared. While the early players and supporters knew each other, lived in the same area and shared a social background, nowadays, anonymity and distant admiration determine the relationship between international stars and local fans.

Although the commodification, commercialization and bourgeoisification of this popular sport happened relatively late, professional football in Germany has developed a formidable and strong commercial axis, but the growing wealth of players, the greed of many football directors, the apparent lack of respect for the local community and the blatant commercialism of the industry has not gone down well with the fans. However, the *Bundesliga* has reasonably fan-friendly attitudes and structures and provides more opportunities for democratic involvement of fans than any other professional football league in Europe.[12]

The demographics of Germany have also changed considerably over the last 100 years. Currently, there are around seven million migrants living in Germany. The largest group of migrants is no longer the Polish but the Turkish community.

Some 3 million people of Turkish origin live in Germany, most of them descendants of Turks invited by the government in the 1950s and 1960s as 'guest workers' to make up for a shortage of manpower [*sic*] after World War II.[13]

However, they tend to be less effectively integrated than other minority groups, are more likely to be poorly educated, often underpaid and disproportionately affected by unemployment.

Similar to the Polish migrants in the 1920s, the large Turkish community in Germany derives from rural areas. They have also developed an extensive network of ethnic clubs and teams. At 'the end of the 1990s, the Turkish community in the largest German federal state, North-Rhine Westphalia, comprised 216 Turkish sports clubs, the largest proportion of the organized milieu after the 445 mosque clubs'.[14] They are very popular and appear to cater successfully for the needs of this minority. Matches often attract large crowds, and teams are frequently sponsored by local Turkish businesses. For Turkish migrants, these clubs provide an opportunity to avoid discrimination, escape social pressures, socialize with other members of the same ethnic background and to avoid isolation. Another important socio-cultural role of these clubs is their ability to offer members and supporters access to a distinct identity and to represent this community publicly. Sporting success can also contribute considerably to a general process of de-stigmatization, particularly if the represented group is widely regarded to be inferior, but proves, in the sporting context, to be (at least) an equal opponent. Although this model of self-organization can increase one's cultural and individual isolation, there appears to be a sense that this model has a positive impact on the self-awareness and self-confidence of those involved. In the past, the German football authorities have either perceived these clubs as a provocation or not acknowledged their existence at all.[15] This is largely a reflection of its rather conservative attitudes and in line with the widespread mantra-like myth that Germany is not a country of immigration. The latter attitude is slowly disappearing in both German society and soccer as the following anecdotes, accounts and analyses will show. These can only be fully understood against the context of these introductory comments that have summarized a small number of significant historical milestones in the development of football in Germany. Without this historical context, it would be very difficult to see that the current situation is the outcome of a lengthy process that started a century ago.

Turkish–Germans vs. German–Turks

In October 2010, Germany played Turkey in Berlin's Olympic Stadium. Thirty thousand Turkish fans, many of them living in Germany's capital, turned out for this Euro 2012 qualifier, which the home team won comfortably 3–0. Man of the Match was the outstanding Mesut Özil. Initially greeted by deafening whistling the Muslim footballer, who recites Qur'an verses before every match, was the most impressive player on the pitch. His goal in the 79th min sealed victory for his team; Germany. Mesut Özil is a third-generation Turkish–German, whose grandfather and father are labour migrants. They came to Germany to offer their family a better life and future. He was born in Gelsenkichen, joined the youth department of Schalke F.C. in 2005, moved to Bremen in 2008 and was transferred to Real Madrid in the summer of 2010. Although Özil is proud of his Turkish roots, background and identity, he opted to play for Germany in recognition of his country of birth and the youth system that had allowed him to excel in soccer.

> Although he was born in the city of Gelsenkirchen in western Germany, Mesut Özil, his older brother and two sisters mostly spoke Turkish at home because their mother didn't understand German well. His father, Mustafa, had come to Germany at the age of two, when Mesut's grandfather got a mining job in the Ruhr Valley. Mesut Özil showed promise as a footballer at a young age, and his father soon began looking after his talented son's affairs.[16]

The Turkish team of that evening also comprised four players who were born and socialized into the world of football in Germany: the twin brothers Hamit and Halil Altintop, both brought up in Wattenscheid, a small town south of Gelsenkirchen; Nuri Sahin, from Lüdenscheid, 28 miles south of Dortmund; and Ömer Erdoğan, who was born and raised in Kassel. All of them decided to have Turkish citizenship, although the first three have spent most of their lives in Germany playing soccer in the *Bundesliga*. Nuri Sahin started to play for Dortmund at the age of 12. Due to his impressive technical talent and composure on the ball, he was promoted to the first team at the tender age of 16. He is still the youngest ever player to feature in Germany's most prestigious league. He joined Real Madrid in 2011, but failed to make an impact and was, subsequently, loaned to English club Liverpool F.C. for the 2012–2013 season. Dortmund replaced Nuri Sahin with another player of Turkish ancestry, Ilkay Gündogan, who plays as a midfielder for both the *Bundesliga* club as well as the German national team. Despite tempting overtures from Turkey, he decided to represent the country of his birth, Germany. Like Mesut Özil he was born and brought up in Gelsenkirchen.[17] Ilkay Gündogan's website contains a large number of photos and references to coal mining, which once defined the town of Gelsenkirchen and offered his grandfather work on his arrival in Germany. In comparison to the Altintop twins, Ilkay Gündogan never played for

Schalke F.C., the Gelsenkirchen-based *Bundesliga* team. Both Altintop brothers started their career in Wattenscheid's local football team. Subsequently, Hamit joined Schalke F.C., Munich, Real Madrid and, most recently, Galatasaray. Halil played for Kaiserslautern, Schalke F.C., Frankfurt and has recently signed a contract with Trabzonsport. Both have been playing for the Turkish national team since 2004.

Since the beginning of this millennium, Turkey's national team has reached the semi-finals of both the 2002 World Cup and Euro 2008. This is largely due to a combination of in-country good quality football and coaching as well as the support from Turkish players abroad. In 1999, the Turkish Football Federation (Türkiye Futbol Federasyonu; TFF) had set up an international scouting system that focused on identifying and recruiting players with Turkish origins in the top European leagues at a very early age.[18] Erdal Keser, a former professional football player of Dortmund (1980–1984 and 1986–1987) and Turkish international (1982–1991), was centrally involved in running this scheme.

The biographies, achievements and successes of Mesut Özil, Nuri Sahin and Ilkay Gündogan are the most visible signs that German football culture has become more diverse and embracing. This applies to both the *Bundesliga* and the German national team and constitutes a major shift from the 1980s and 1990s. These decades are often remembered for the disturbing public displays of racist and xenophobic attitudes in the context of international matches.[19] Weeks before a game against Turkey in 1983, a flyer was distributed in several German football grounds. It accused Turkish migrants of stealing 'German jobs' and 'flooding the country'. It also threatened the Turkish population with violence. Consequently, 5000 police officers were gathered to ensure the safety of the Turkish team and its supporters. However, on the night of the match, the Olympic Stadium in Berlin was only half filled with hardly any Turkish fans in the stands. Considering the popularity of this sport among Turkish migrants and the considerable size of the Turkish community in Berlin, the absence of Turkish spectators clearly indicated widespread fear. This example is just one of many that demonstrates the racism and xenophobia in German football in the 1980s and 1990s[20] and the links to out-dated nationalist attitudes. It also offers an explanation that accounts for the absence of Turkish players in the German *Bundesliga* during these decades. The few Turkish players who had been enlisted by professional teams in Germany were frequently subjected to racist and xenophobic abuse. They usually took the first opportunity to transfer 'home' to join a professional club in Turkey.

On the pitch: The United Nations of Germany?

The composition of the German side that played Turkey in 2010 and, later, competed in Euro 2012 offers more valuable insights into the more embracing attitude of Germans and the redefined sense of Germanness in the twenty-first century. Lukas Podolski and Miroslav Klose are Polish-born forwards and important players for Germany's national soccer team. Sami Khedira's father is Tunisian. Like Mesut Özil, he is a practicing Muslim. Mario Gomez has a Spanish mother and Jerome Boateng's father is Ghanaian. Cacau was born in São Paulo, Brazil. He received German citizenship in February 2009 after living and working in Germany for eight years. Marko Marin was born in Bosnia. In total, eleven of the 23 players had foreign roots. This colourful mix of the current German national team is the result of some major policy changes in the country at the turn of the century that made it easier for migrants and their children to gain citizenship. Since 2000, a child is by law entitled to a German passport if one of the parents has been living in Germany for at least eight years. Consequently, after Euro 2008, Germany's manager, Joachim Löw, was able to not only rejuvenate his squad but put together the most ethnically diverse team ever.[21]

By doing that, Löw threw out the old stereotypes about German football, in particular, the deeply ingrained cliché of Teutonic efficiency. He introduced a playing style that suits these new players and is clearly influenced by them. Germany's traditional and conventional approach, which has often been compared to a hard-working, determined and well-oiled but heavy-going machine, has been replaced by a creative and attractive playing style that tends be more commonly associated with South American teams.

> Up front, we exude a bit of Latin or southern ease but defensively, we are incredibly disciplined, very German,' said Khedira. Özil noted that 'my technique and feeling for the ball is the Turkish side to my game and the always-give-your-all attitude is the German part' while Aogo said that 'the mixture of African physical strength and European tactical awareness can be very good for the DFB.[22]

This new face and style of football has been widely appreciated in German society, with only a few exceptions. Of course, Löw's young team faced opposition from the far right for being 'un-German' and from a popular tabloid paper, which criticized individual players for lacking passion when singing the national anthem. Its back-page headline even asked: 'Are we patriotic enough?'

> The right-wing NPD (the equivalent of the BNP) produced a calendar with a picture of the national shirt with Owomoyela's squad number on it and the slogan: 'White: not just the colour of the shirt! For a real National team!' The leader of the party was taken to court by Owomoyela and the German FA and found guilty of inciting racial hatred and given a seven-month suspended sentence.[23]

There is little doubt that the composition of the German national side is accompanied by timely and useful reflections about the country's identity as the old certainties of one's nationality have become more flexible and blurred. The question remains whether the popularity of outstanding players like Özil and Khedira is a genuine sign that German society is relinquishing some of its prejudices, becoming more tolerant and gradually embracing its multi-cultural and multi-national composition or whether their presence is a political virtue born out of a practical necessity.

The German national team performed dismally at the 1998 World Cup in France and Euro 2000, the latter their worst overall performance in a major tournament since World War II.[24] This unusual string of unsuccessful and disappointing performances led to an emotionally and ideologically loaded search for reasons. The public discourse quickly identified a large number of scapegoats: the foreign players in the *Bundesliga*. Conservative forces saw German society and the country's glorified football system as the victim of a 'foreigner flood' (*Ausländerschwemme*). However, Ottmar Hitzfeld, a Maths and Physical Education teacher and one of the most successful *Bundesliga* managers, who won several national and international titles with both Dortmund and Munich, was one of the first to challenge that simplistic and undifferentiated view. He pointed out the obvious that Germany's talent pool was poor, with very few young players emerging, and needed more careful nurturing. He suggested paying more attention to the large number of gifted young players who were born, brought up and living in Germany but not eligible to play for the country of their birth due to the outdated citizenship laws. France's glamorous and victorious World Cup campaign in 1998 offered plenty of convincing evidence and support for Hitzfeld's argument. The French team was full of outstanding players of ethnic minorities that showed both competency and flair. They were also acclaimed for their multiculturalism, and how they symbolized a new, inclusive France that embraced all ethnic groups.

Eventually, a major rational rethink about the development of young players led to a fundamental overhaul of the football academy structures in 2002 and a € 500m investment in order to restructure fully the youth development system. The revamped, centrally controlled scheme required all 36 clubs in the two *Bundesliga* divisions to operate youth academies. If they fail to comply, they are not provided with the license that allows them to compete in these leagues. At any one time, approximately, 5000 players go through the system. Boys are taken on from the age of 12. Furthermore, these academies have to ensure that, per annual intake, at least 12 players must be eligible to compete for Germany. The result of this new system is impressive. At the 2010 South Africa World Cup, Germany fielded one of the youngest sides, with an average age of 24.7 years. All 23 members of the German squad had come through the youth academies. The annual investment of € 80 m also had an impact on the composition of the *Bundesliga*, as currently almost two thirds of the players are eligible to play for the national team.

> Over the past 11 years, according to the *Bundesliga*, German clubs have invested an impressive $650 million in youth development. In that time, the percentage of Germans in the Bundesliga has risen from 50 to 57 percent as the average age of German players in the top division has fallen from 27.9 to 25.8 years old. By the end of the 2010–2011 *Bundesliga* season, 52.4 percent of the players in the league had graduated from a German youth academy, with 20.4 percent of those players playing for the first team of the club they joined as youngsters.[25]

These youth academies also make significant contributions to the integration of foreigners and are very popular with the male offspring of labour migrants who were born in Germany. A recent study by a European Business School found that the *Bundesliga* academies host boys from more than 80 countries. However, a considerable proportion of these youngsters were born and brought up in Germany. They will, therefore, one day be able to choose whether they wish to play for their country of birth or one of the 30 countries from which their parents originated.[26] The same study argues that this group shows a particularly strong identification with German culture and society. Anecdotal evidence also suggests that young players from migrant families are more committed, better motivated and driven by the desire to climb the social ladder via sporting success than their German peers.

Off the pitch: German and Germany fans

From the 1980s to the mid-1990s, the sub-cultural style of young German football fans was largely a mirror image of their English counterparts.[27] Many of their first chants were translations of English songs and the first mass-produced scarves that were sold in Germany were manufactured in Britain.[28] From the mid-1990s onwards, German fans increasingly incorporated sub-cultural practices of the Italian

Ultras in their behaviour. This is closely linked to a major generational shift on German football terraces,[29] the far-ranging changes English football went through in the early 1990s, in particular the compulsory introduction of all-seater stadia from 1992, and the increased media coverage of Italian football.

The behaviour of German fans in the context of international football matches during the 1980s and 1990s is best summarized as a combination of aggressive and often violent expression of masculinity and the exaggerated celebration of the nation. The latter tended to be driven by the illusion of an ethnically homogenous nation-state. This explosive mixture received a considerable boost through German re-unification and the subsequent uncritical celebration of *Volk und Vaterland* (people and fatherland) by politicians of all major parties. The threat of potential rioting led to the cancellation of two international matches: the first against a selection of East-German players in December 1990 to celebrate the re-unification of German football, and the other against England in 1994, originally scheduled for 20 April, Adolf Hitler's birthday. Planning a friendly against England on that date clearly displays a high degree of political naivity and a lack of historical sensitivity within the German Football Association (Deutscher Fussballbund, DFB). However, such ineptness is, arguably, an integral part of the political history of this governing body.[30]

It does not come as a surprise, therefore, that the biographies of the very small number of black players who were selected for the West-German national team during this period frequently mention racist abuse on and off the pitch. Erwin Kostedde made his debut in 1974. Although he played only three times for West-Germany, he opened the door for the next generation of black talent to break through. The second black player to join the national squad, in 1979, was William (Jimmy) Hartwig. The first black player to score for Germany was Gerald Asamoah, who was born in Ghana (1978) but moved to Germany at the age of 12 and gained citizenship in 2001. Capped 43 times, the striker was part of two German World Cup campaigns, in 2002 and 2006 and became the target of a different racist campaign of the NPD. On several occasions, they distributed stickers saying 'No, Gerald, you are not Germany – you are the FRG', emphasizing the formal element of Asamoah's citizenship and, at the same time, excluding him from, what the far right perceives as the truly German people (*deutsches Volk*).

Against this disconcerting historical backdrop, the developments over the last ten years are impressive and promising. Since the 2002 World Cup, co-hosted by Japan and South Korea, the German flag has become a popular emblem that embraces class, creed and colour. Never before in the sporting and political history of this country have so many black-red-golden flags been waved, fixed to cars, been displayed in windows, used to decorate the streets, and sewn onto clothes. This is the same flag that, since its reinstatement in 1945, had been flying mostly over old, stuffy, official state and government buildings, to highlight their importance or to honour the dead. While in the past this banner has been largely ignored, nowadays, it has become an unlikely partner in the creation and celebration of a modified sense of Germanness. The fact that so many people from a vast range of backgrounds wrap themselves in this abstract emblem demonstrates a new and modern sense of national identity and a playful, non-threatening patriotism that continues to stun the world.

Equally striking, in this respect, was the 2006 World Cup that the Germans hosted. Participating teams, travelling fans, journalists and high-profile politicians, including Kofi Annan and Tony Blair, judged this event as being one of the best ever World Cups.[31] There are a host of reasons for this generally positive feedback from across the world: firstly, the Germans confirmed that they could plan, prepare and manage a decent party, but the World Cup also showed that the German people could be fun-loving hedonists. Over one month, the country revelled in its biggest and most enjoyable festival since the fall of the Berlin Wall. Secondly, Germany presented itself as a confident, creative and hospitable place where visiting fans, -foreigners and minority groups were not segregated but encouraged to mix. Fans from abroad without tickets were not treated suspiciously or sent home but were given a warm reception. They were encouraged to stay and watch matches on giant screens, which had been put up in almost every city and town centre in the country, for free. Some observers concluded that 'Germany 2006 was the most 'fan'-oriented event in the tournament's 76 year history'.[32] Thirdly, Germany's often uninspired, mechanistic and dull football victories of the past had been a precise reflection of the country's self-image and its desperate attempts to not put a foot wrong.[33] The new, more attractive and somewhat successful playing style clearly reflected wider changes, in particular the discovery of a healthy, confident and non-threatening patriotism.[34] As in 2002, millions of Germans publicly embraced the national flag and decorated various objects with it. Wigs in the colours of Germany were as popular as tricoloured face paintings. Fourthly, in the past, this overwhelming wave of national feeling and patriotism would have caused a media-orchestrated public outcry of indignation and anger abroad, reminding the Germans of their Nazi past. On this occasion, the international media hailed German citizen and football fans for their soft and playful brand of patriotism.

Euro 2012 was no exception, despite one minor incident that caused widespread concern. A small group of fans was criticized for chanting 'Sieg – Sieg' (victory) in Lviv, Ukraine, when the German squad played Denmark. This chant has been condemned for its association with the Nazi greeting of 'Sieg Heil'. It is particularly tasteless due to the suffering of both Poland and Ukraine at the hands of the German armed forces in World War II. Overall, however, the well-behaved German fans and their light-hearted patriotism have become popular with the media, who appear to be keen to project a softer image of Germanness these days. Television viewers around the world witnessed the image of a female German fan crying after Germany conceded the second goal against Italy in the semi-finals of Euro 2012. However, it turned out that this short clip had been recorded shortly before the start of the match during the playing of the national anthems. The producers, UEFA TV, inserted these tears into the 'live' coverage that was supplied to television audiences all over the world.

In Berlin, half a million Germany fans saw both the match and the tears on vast outdoor screens at the Brandenburg Gate. The venue and attendance in Germany's capital was the largest of approximately 100 public viewing areas throughout the country. In Cologne, almost 35,000 supporters came together to partake remotely in Germany's semi-final clash with Italy, in Frankfurt's *Fan Park* 30,000 people gathered and in Dortmund 18,000 hoped for their unbeaten team to advance to the final of Euro 2012. Most of these public viewing areas were free and set up by local councils.

There are two different types: first, the so-called *Fan Parks* that are spatially confined and have a maximum capacity; and second, those that are not limited in the number of people attending as they cover main roads, huge parks or spacious squares. Haferburg et al claim that these venues need to be understood as the extension of one's lounge onto the pavement, where 'the boundaries between public and private spheres merge'.[35] All of them have a festival and party-like atmosphere in common. Some do not only offer football but enhance the experience with live music, light entertainment and other performances before and after the match, and through the provision of solid and liquid refreshments. They do not only attract traditional male German football supporters but also appeal to women, children, families, foreigners, migrants and minorities. One of the most important differences between the public viewing areas and the stadium is the degree of freedom and mobility that visitors can enjoy. Restrictions and policing are minimal, there is no allocated seating, fans are not spatially segregated and moving around during the match is wholly acceptable.

And yet, the excitement, the group experience and identification, the support of one's team through colourful flags and outfits, chants and whistling, the emotional roller coasters are very similar to the experience within the football grounds. Most visitors I spoke to suggested that public viewing areas combine the best of both worlds, watching football in a convenient domestic environment and being part of a match live in a stadium. Eastman and Land even suggest that 'television viewing in public serves special participatory and social needs not wholly met in either the home or the stadium context'.[36]

During Euro 2012, my observations confirmed that the ethnic mix, youth, flair and cultural practices of the diverse fans and spectators in the *Fan Parks* and other public viewing areas continued to portray Germany as a confident, creative and multicultural place. As before, this tournament offered German fans an opportunity to celebrate a new sense of Germanness underpinned by a non-threatening and playful patriotism. The national parochialism has disappeared and has been replaced by a more relaxed and undogmatic sense of pride.

Having undertaken several ethnographic visits, which involved observing and interviewing visitors, to the public viewing area in Dortmund during Euro 2012, there is little doubt that it is the combination of the carnivalesque, party-like atmosphere and support for their team that motivated the predominantly young people to attend this venue. Argot, image and demeanor of the vast majority of fans is very similar to those in German football stadia, although the exaggerated celebration of masculinity is missing. This might be caused by the very different socio-demographic composition that contains a significantly larger number of women and children in attendance. Although the chanting, cheering, singing and whistling is less intense and coordinated than in a stadium, watching a match in public offers these fans a unique and collective experience. This is underpinned and enhanced by the sociability that the spatial arrangements of these public viewing area scater for. There appears to be a clear shift from the closeness to the event to the closeness of the experience, with high levels of excitement and emotional involvement. Due to the significant geographical distance between the team and the fans, the latter are unable actively to contribute to the creation of a sports spectacle. However, the spectacle that football supporters in public viewing areas create is an impressive visual feast, charismatic in its own distinct way and fostering a sense of community that is more versatile and inclusive than in football grounds.

Another striking element of these public viewing areas is the lack of any segregation between different fan groups, the constant movement of people and, during Euro 2012, the mixing of supporters of different countries who could be easily identified by their flags, clothes and face paintings. In addition to traditional market-like stalls selling merchandise of all the teams competing in Euro 2012, face paintings, in various national colours and colour combinations, could be purchased on site. The latter was particularly popular with children, who appeared to choose certain colour combinations regardless of their national affiliations. When Germany's matches were shown, the public viewing area in Dortmund turned into a sea of black, red and gold. When other games were broadcast, the area in front of the giant screen turned into an even more colourful panoramaas most people were waving both the flag of the team they supported and the German colours.

This kind of hybridity can also be found on the terraces of some *Bundesliga* stadiums where, for example, flags have become more imaginative and reflect a cosmopolitan outlook. Whilst traditionally many fans held and waved small copies of the official, industrially produced club's flag, nowadays they are often complex examples of hand-made patch work. The dominant feature is obviously the colour combination of one's team and its official emblem and/or the club's name. Many fans, however, have added other important symbols. Particularly popular are the official flags of the native countries of the foreign players.

In Dortmund, the Polish flag is particularly popular. It is a powerful reminder of the close and long historical relationship between the Ruhr area and Polish migrants. It also acknowledges that, currently, Borussia Dortmund hosts three outstanding Polish internationals: Robert Lewandowski, Jakub Blaszczykowski, also known as 'Kuba', and Lukasz Piszczek. At the end of the 2011–2012 *Bundesliga* season, the soccer magazine *Kicker* rated them as among the top eight players of Germany's highest division. In 2010, Robert Lewandowski became the most expensive Polish player ever, when Poznan sold the young striker to Dortmund for € 4.5 m. At Euro 2012, Polish hopes rested largely on the shoulders of these three players, who the media frequently and proudly refer to as *Polonia Dortmund*. Considering that Nazi Germany instigated World War II with the invasion of Poland in September 1939, German–Polish football relations appear to be unequivocally relaxed. This can only be fully understood in the wider context of a long history of labour migration from Poland to the Ruhr area, which this paper addressed earlier.

> Dortmund and the surrounding area have been a Polish stomping ground since the days of the German Kaiser. They immigrated here to work in the coal mines and steel mills, and the names of their descendents, such as Tilkowski and Kwiatkowski, now adorn the Borussia hall of fame. The priest of the Polish Catholic mission in Dortmund has 32 Lewandowskis in his registry. They now often see their namesake, the Borussia striker, attending Mass in St Anna's Church ... To the great amusement of many, Klopp (Borussia Dortmund's manager. U.M.) has recently taken to yelling 'Rusz dupe!' ('Move your ass!') as an occasional demonstration of his proficiency in Polish. Even the groundskeeper is from Poland and known for circulating jokes about his own countrymen.[37]

The three Dortmund Poles will certainly join Borussia's hall of fame as they were pivotal in the team's two successive *Bundesliga* titles in 2011 and 2012 and the relatively successful Champions League campaign in 2012–2013. They will not be the first Poles to receive that kind of honour as Dortmund's team boosts a long history of absorbing players with Polish roots who have enriched the team's diversity and quality.

Conclusion

In 2008, Diethelm Blecking observed that the majority of outstanding Turkish–German football players had opted to play for Turkey, rather than the German national team. He concludes that this trend is a clear reflection of the 'dismal relationship between German majority and Turkish minority' but acknowledges that it also provides evidence of the 'powerful impact of Turkish nationalism'.[38] Only five years later, that trend is no longer that unequivocal. Both on and off the football pitch, there have been some significant changes. The ethnic diversity of Germany's current national squad and the cultural practices of both German and Germany fans are powerful reflections of a modified understanding, interpretation and sense of Germanness that is increasingly underpinned by a largely non-threatening, playful and inclusive patriotism. It appears that the steady flow of migrants into Germany after World War II has helped considerably to re-define and modernize the concept of Germanness. While the old, traditional and conservative version of national identity suffered from a lack of popularity and was even treated with suspicion and caution, the reconstructed, modern and increasingly inclusive notion of Germanness appears to be more widely accepted, fashionable and publicly celebrated.

There are at least three key factors that, combined, offer an explanation of this development that affects both German society as well as the world of soccer: First, there have been some major policy changes in Germany at the beginning of the new millennium that have made it easier for immigrants and their offspring to gain citizenship. Second, in 2002, the German soccer authorities implemented a new youth development system that was intended to promote local talent that will be eligible to play for Germany irrespective of ethnic background. Third, after Euro 2008, the Germany manager, Joachim Löw, has not only revitalized and rejuvenated his squad but also put together the most ethnically diverse team ever. The chronological order of political and football events inevitably suggests that the increased ethnic diversity that currently characterizes the composition of the national team is the outcome and result of wider socio-political change. Mesut Özil's story is particularly important, as the Turkish-German community constitutes the largest minority in Germany. While the Altintop brothers opted to play for the country of their parents, he has chosen to compete for his country of birth, which could inspire others to follow his example. The question as to what extent the multi-culturalism of Germany's football ambassadors impacts on German society, and its acceptance of minority groups, in general, needs to be tackled next.

In addition to the socio-political aspects of this recent development, there are also implications for the playing style of the German team that has become more attractive, more attacking and more appreciated. Interestingly, the composition of this squad is not a reflection of a colonial past but a model of contemporary German society.

This development is part of wider processes of social change that a minority of right-wing political forces continue to resist and undermine. While they firmly hold on to the outdated belief in an ethnically homogenous German nation that does not offer a permanent home for migrants, the vast majority of Germans acknowledges and accepts that most of these migrants will stay. After all, Germany has a diverse history of immigration that can be traced back for more than a century.

Notes

1. Merkel, 'Politics of Physical Culture and German Nationalism', 69–96.
2. Pflaum, *Die Kultur-Zivilisations-AntitheseimDeutschen*, 288.
3. Eisenberg, 'Deutschland', 94–129.
4. Dixon, 'Prussia, Politics and Physical Education', 134–5.
5. Lindner and Breuer, *Sind dochnichtalles Beckenbauers*, 9.
6. Lindner and Breuer, *Sind dochnichtalles Beckenbauers*, 11.
7. Eisenberg, 'Deutschland', 94–129.
8. Gehrmann, *Fußball – Vereine – Politik*, 37–67.
9. Lindner and Breuer, *Sind dochnichtalles Beckenbauers*, 35–7.
10. Blecking, 'Sport and Immigration in Germany', 958.
11. Merkel, 'Football Made in Germany', 93–118.
12. Merkel, 'Football Fans and Clubs in Germany', 359–76.
13. Gezer and Reimann, 'Erdogan Urges Turks Not to Assimilate', 30.
14. Blecking, 'Sport and Immigration in Germany', 964.
15. Blecking, 'Fußball und ethnischer Sport in Deutschland', 90.
16. Kramer, 'On the Verge of Greatness', 33.
17. Heering, *Fussball Bundesliga: 50 Jahre*, 99–102.
18. Kroner, 'Multikultifür Deutschland', 24.
19. Merkel, 'Football Identity and Youth Culture in Germany', 52–66.
20. Merkel, Sombert, and Tokarski, 'Racism and Xenophobia in Germany', 143–68.
21. Connolly, 'Germans Celebrate the Diversity of Their "multiculti" Team', 33.
22. Hytner, 'World Cup 2010: Germany Reap the Rewards', 23
23. White, 'Germany v Australia: Mesut Özil at Head of the Vanguard', 16.
24. Schulze-Marmeling and Dahlkamp, 'Deutsche Tugenden', 451–78.
25. Bienkowski, 'Euro 2012: Germany has Changed', 10.
26. European Business School, *Integration through Professional Football.*
27. Redhead, 'An Era of the End, or the End of an Era: Football and Youth Culture', 160–86.
28. Gabriel, *Ultra Bewegungen in Deutschland*, 180.
29. Scheidle, 'Ultra (recht)s in Italien,' 92 claims that the vast majority of German Ultras are aged between 16 and 24 years.
30. Heinrich, *Der Deutsche Fussballbund*. Merkel, 'The Hidden History of the German Football Association', 167–86.
31. Harding, 'How to Win at Football', 24.
32. Frew and McGillivray, 'Exploring Hyper-experiences', 187.
33. Merkel, 'Football Made in Germany', 101.
34. Biermann, 'Trains Running Late and Football with Flair', 7.
35. Haferburg, Golka, and Selter, 'Public Viewing Areas: Urban Interventions', 174–99.
36. Eastman and Land, 'The Best of Two Worlds', 175.
37. Buschmann and Mayr, 'The Magic Trio', 35.
38. Blecking, *Fussball and ethnischer Sport in Deutschland*, 93.

References

Bienkowski, S. 'Euro 2012: Germany has Changed. England Take Note'. *The New York Times*, June 4, 2012, 10.

Biermann, C. 'Trains Running Late and Football with Flair – We'll Do Anything to Fit in'. *The Guardian*, June 25, 2006, 7.

Blecking, D. 'Sport and Immigration in Germany'. *The International Journal of the History of Sport* 25, no. 8 (2008): 955–73.

Blecking, D. 'Fußball and Ethnischer Sport in Deutschland' [Football and ethnic sports in Germany]. In *Sport – Ethnie – Nation: Zur Geschichte und Soziologie des Sports in nationalitaten konflickten und bei Minoritaeten* [Sport – ethnicity – Nation: History and Sociology of Sport in the Context of National Conflicts and Minorities], ed. D. Diethelm Blecking and Marek Waic, 85–95. Baltmannsweiler: Schneider Verlag Hohengehren, 2008.

Buschmann, R., and Walter Mayr. 'The Magic Trio Polish Hopes Rest on: German League Stars at Euro 2012'. *Der Spiegel*, May 30, 2012, 35.

Connolly, K. 'Germans Celebrate the Diversity of Their "multiculti" World Cup Team'. *The Guardian*, June 27, 2010, 33.

Dixon, J.G. 'Prussia, Politics and Physical Education'. In *Landmarks in the History of Physical Education*, ed. Peter McIntosh and John Dixon, 112–55. London: RKP, 1986.

Eastman, S.T., and A.M. Land. 'The Best of Both Worlds: Sports Fans Find Good Seats at the Bar'. *Journal of Sport and Social Issues* 21, no. 2 (1997): 156–78.

Eisenberg, C. 'Deutschland' [Germany]. In *Fussball – Soccer – Calico. Einenglischer Sport auf dem Weg um die Welt* [Football – An English sport travelling the world], ed. Christiane Eisenberg, 94–129. Munich: dtv, 1997.

European Business School. *Integration through Professional Football*. European Business School: Oestrich-Winkel, 2010.

Frew, M., and D. McGillivra. 'Exploring Hyper-experiences: Performing the Fan at Germany 2006'. *Journal of Sport and Tourism* 13, no. 3 (2008): 181–98.

Gabriel, M. 'Ultra Bewegungen in Deutschland; Von Doppelhaltern und Choreografien – die Antwort der Kurve auf den Fußballals Event' [The ultra movement in Germany. The response of the stands to football as an event]. In *Ballbesitzist Diebstahl – Fans zwischen Kultur und Kommerz* [Ball ownership is theft – Fans between culture and commerce], ed. Bündnis Aktiver Fußball fans, 179–94. Göttingen: Verlag Die Werkstatt, 2004.

Gehrmann, S. *Fußball-Vereine-Politik. Zur Sportgeschichte des Reviers* [Football–Clubs–Politics, The history of sport in the Ruhr area]. Essen: Reimar Hobbing Verlag, 1988.

Gezer, Ö., and A. Reimann. 'Erdogan Urges Turks Not to Assimilate: "You are part of Germany, but also part of our great Turkey"'. *The Spiegel*, February 28, 2011, 30.

Haferburg, C., T. Golka, and S. Selter. 'Public Viewing Areas: Urban Interventions in the Context of Mega Events'. In *Development and Dreams: Urban Legacy of the 2010 Football World Cup*, ed. Udesh Pillay, Richard Tomlinson, and Orli Bass, 174–99. Cape Town: HSRC Press, 2009.

Harding, L. 'How to Win at Football'. *The Guardian*, July 10, 2006, 24.

Heering, K. *Fussball Bundesliga: 50 Jahre* [German Bundesliga: 50 years]. Munich: Arsedition, 2012.

Heinrich, A. Der *Deutsche Fußballbund – Einepolitische Geschichte* [The German football Association: A political history]. Köln: PapyRossa, 2000.

Hesse-Lichtenberger, U. *Tor! – The Story of German Football*. London: WSC Books, 2003.

Hytner, D. 'World Cup 2010: Germany Reap the Rewards of the Liberation Generation'. *The Guardian*, June 17, 2010, 23.

Kramer, J. 'On the Verge of Greatness: Germany's Shy Football Prodigy Mesut Özil'. *Der Spiegel*, June 27, 2012, 33.

Kröner, A. 'Multikultifür Deutschland'. *Der Spiegel*, June 18, 2004, 24.

Lindner, R., and H.T. Breuer. *Sind dochnichtalles Beckenbauers* [Not all of them are Beckenbauers]. Frankfurt: Syndicat Verlag, 1982.

Merkel, U. 'Football Made in Germany: Solid, Reliable and Undramatic but Successful'. In *Hosts and Champions – Football Cultures, National Identities and the World Cup in the USA*, ed. John Sugden and Alan Tomlinson, 93–118. Avebury: Gower Press, 1994.

Merkel, U. 'Football Identity and Youth Culture in Germany'. In *Football Cultures and Identities*, ed. Gary Armstrong and Richard Giulianotti, 52–66. London: MacMillan, 1999.

Merkel, U. 'The Hidden History of the German Football Association (DFB): 1900–1950'. *Soccer and Society* 1, no. 2 (2000): 167–86.

Merkel, U. 'The Politics of Physical Culture and German Nationalism: *Turnen* versus English Sports and French Olympism'. *German Politics and Society* 21, no. 2 (2003): 69–96.

Merkel, U. 'Football Fans and Clubs in Germany: Conflicts, Crises and Compromises'. *Soccer and Society* 13, no. 3 (2012): 171–88.

Merkel, U., K. Sombert, and W. Tokarski. 'Football, Racism and Xenophobia in Germany: 50 Years Later – Here We Go Again?' In *Racism and Xenophobia in European Football*, ed. Udo Merkel and Walter Tokarski, 143–68. Aachen: Meyer and Meyer, 1996.

Pflaum, M. 'Die Kultur-Zivilisations-Antitheseim Deutschen' [The antithesis of culture and civilization in German]. In *Europäische Schlüsselwörter. Wortvergleicheund wortges-*

chichtliche Studien [Key European words: Word comparisons and historical studies], ed. Jürgen Knobloch, 288–427. Munich: Hueber, 1967.

Redhead, S. 'An Era of the End, or the End of an Era: Football and Youth Culture'. In *British Football and Social Change – Getting into Europe*, ed. John Williams and Stephen Wagg, 145–59. Leicester: Leicester University Press, 1991.

Scheidle, J. 'Ultra (recht) s in Italien' [Ultra (right) in Italy]. In *Tatort Stadion – Rassismus, Antisemitismus und Sexismusim Fußball* [Crime scene stadium: Racism, anti-semitism and sexism in football], ed. Gerd Dembowski and Jürgen Scheidle, 90–109. Köln: Papy Rossa Verlag, 2002.

Schulze-Marmeling, D., and H. Dahlkamp. 'Deutsche Tugenden' [German Virtues]. In *Die Geschichte der Fußball Nationalmannschaft* [The history of the German national team], ed. Dietrich Schulze-Marmeling, 415–78. Göttingen: Verlag Die Werkstatt, 2004.

White, D. 'Germany v Australia: Mesut Özil at Head of the Vanguard for New Generation'. *The Telegraph*, June 12, 2010, 16.

Poles apart: foreign players, Polish football and Euro 2012

Richard Elliott and Konrad Bania

[a]Lawrie McMenemy Centre for Football Research, Southampton Solent University, Southampton, UK; [b]University of Liverpool, Liverpool, UK

The 14th running of the UEFA European Championships represented a watershed moment for football, and sport more broadly, in Eastern Europe. Whilst the competition itself might have been restricted to Europe's elite national teams, world football's gaze was drawn towards the joint hosts, Poland and the Ukraine, for the duration of the tournament. At this juncture, therefore, this paper seeks to consider the 'place' of football in Eastern Europe, and in this case, Poland specifically, by conducting an analysis of the economic value of Poland's top division – the Ekstraklasa, and by examining the factors that influence foreign players' decisions to migrate to that particular league. The paper identifies that whilst the Ekstraklasa might sit outside of Europe's core football economies, it still offers much as a migration destination for certain sorts of players. However, the paper also shows that whilst the 2012 UEFA European Championships provided significant exposure for Poland in the football context, it is less clear if hosting the event will have a lasting effect on the development of Poland's top league and its desirability to foreign players.

Introduction

The 14th running of the UEFA European Championships represented a watershed moment for football, and sport more broadly, in Eastern Europe. To date, most sports mega-events have been held in what might be described as 'developed' nations.[1] However, more recently, developing, emerging and transitional economies have been more successful in bidding for, and hosting, events of this nature. In football, the most recent examples include the 2002 and 2010 FIFA World Cups that were held in Japan and Korea, and South Africa respectively, and the 2012 UEFA European Championships, jointly hosted by Poland and the Ukraine. Arguably, the awarding of these major football events to these emerging or transitional football nations is a reflection of the increasingly conscious attempts being made by the game's governing authorities to globalize the sport outside of what are commonly recognized as the game's core economies.

In professional football, the core economies are located in Western Europe where the game's 'big-five' European leagues are situated. The English Premier League, Spanish La Liga, Italian Serie A, German Bundesliga and French Ligue 1 generally command the greatest media interest, the broadest fan bases and the highest revenues.[2] Within these leagues exist some of the world's richest sports brands, including Manchester United and Liverpool in England, Real Madrid and Barcelona in Spain, and Bayern Munich in Germany.

Clearly, not all of Europe's football teams or football leagues can be located at the core of the game's global economy, however; the globalization of football, like other facets of life in a globalized world, has not been even over time. Political, economic and cultural factors have all influenced the permeation of the global sport *par excellence*[3] into different parts of Europe (and the world) at different times. Moreover, it should not be assumed that the globalisation of football and the relative (economic) success of some teams and leagues should be seen to reflect the economic success of nations in broader terms; some of the world's most powerful economies are located outside of football's economic core.[4]

Given the above, it is not our intention to examine one of European football's elite leagues in this paper. Instead, we focus on what might be referred to as a transitional economy in football terms – the Polish Ekstraklasa. We do this for two reasons; firstly, to make some sense of the Ekstraklasa's place in football's European order post-Euro 2012, and secondly, to better understand why migrant players might select the Ekstraklasa as their migration destination when, in many cases, migrations are more likely to flow towards core economies.[5] To begin to make sense of these objectives, the first part of the paper examines the movements of workers in football.

Migration in football

The contemporary globalisation of sport has been marked by the increasing numbers of athletes who, for any number of reasons, migrate from their country of birth to ply their athletic labour. Most, if not all, elite sports leagues and competitions now host athletes and other workers from a broad cross-section of places and movements within professional football are no different. Therefore, whilst there is a certain amount of truth in the contention that migration in football is as old as the game itself,[6] it has predominantly been in the last 20 years that intensification in the globalisation of football labour has become more evident.[7]

The reasons for the increase in migratory movements are reflective of a series of interdependent processes, some of which are specific to football and others that are manifest in broader processes of globalisation. For example, at a general level, the ability to traverse the globe with relative ease has made places that, until relatively recently, seemed distant, appear close. Moreover, technological advancement, in recent times driven by internet-based technologies, has made global communication cheaper and easier. In football, the increasing commercialisation of the game at the elite level, driven, in part, by the developing relationships between sponsors, advertisers and the media, has resulted in the exponential growth in salaries for elite players plying their trade in Europe's core economies.[8] The 1995 Bosman ruling also significantly impacted the mobility of players[9] and influenced the salaries that they can command.

An analysis of the changing financial structure of professional football (especially in Europe's big-five leagues) highlights the significant growth in club and league revenues, media rights sales, player valuations and salary costs.[10] The rise in salary costs is particularly significant given that some European leagues have witnessed enormous salary growth in the last 20 years. The increase in salaries has led some scholars to argue that the major influencing factor in determining a player's decision to migrate is the 'mercenary' desire to secure the greatest financial reward that can be offered by a club.[11] Outside of professional sport, such contentions would seem sensible, given that migration often occurs to take advantage of positive wage disparities.[12]

Whilst the desire to command the highest salary may influence a player's decision to migrate, it is rarely the only antecedent to a player's move, however. As Maguire and Pearton have identified, the practice of 'following the money'[13] is interconnected with a broader series of processes that reflect political, historical, cultural and geographical patterns. In this respect, research that has examined the motives behind the movements of professional footballers has identified that a range of interdependent processes contour the decision to migrate. These include the need to seek out a professional sporting experience, an intensity of commitment, the desire to test one's abilities at the highest level and the capacity to take advantage of cultural similarities such as language familiarity.[14] Additionally, Magee and Sugden[15] have shown that migration does not always occur by choice. On some occasions, players may be pushed from a particular location, they might be exiled or expelled from the league or even the country in which they currently ply their trade.

This latter point is interesting, specifically in the context of push factors where a player might not be presented with a full range of choices from which to select their migration destination. Whilst we are not suggesting here that the migrants examined in this paper are in some way exiled or expelled as in Magee and Sugden's context, we are suggesting that their range of options may be limited for one reason or another. This is an important point, because, as Carter[16] points out, not all athletic migrants are part of a 'free moving cosmopolitan population who strategically engage in migration to further careers and earn significant wealth'. Therefore, for the migrants being examined in this paper, it is important to make sense of the pull *and* push factors that often contour migration decisions; issues that include, for example, the overproduction of athletic labour and the resultant flooding of leagues in different parts of the world. This has presented a problem for workers in sports such as basketball and ice hockey where migration to England, for example, is marked by North American 'ambitionist'[17] -type migrants who would otherwise struggle to find professional playing opportunities in the National Basketball Association (NBA), National Hockey League (NHL) or in the more established European leagues.[18]

Push factors also include the lack of opportunity for career development in a player's home-nation. This has been seen to be the case in the migration of North American football (soccer) players out of the American sporting space.[19] Additionally, the increasingly commonplace migrations of African players to leagues in Europe can often be identified as the result of a lack of opportunities in the various leagues located on the continent.[20] Whilst there are a number of very good club sides located in African nations, for many African players, these clubs simply do not match their level of ability or desire.

Taking these factors into account, it is argued that the motivations of the migrants being examined in this paper cannot be reduced to any single causal factor. Indeed, their decision to migrate should not simply be reduced to a series of intrinsic and largely personal influences. To be truly meaningful, the various structural concerns, or push factors, should also be taken into consideration, along with the more personal determinants of the motivation to migrate. Only when this combination of factors is considered can some observations be made with respect to the migrant motivations under examination in this particular context. To help make sense of the structural determinants evident in the decisions of players migrating to Poland's Ekstraklasa, the next part of the paper seeks to place the league in football's European order post Euro 2012.

Polish football, the Ekstraklasa and Euro-2012

It was during the late1980s that the transition from communist state to capitalist system with parliamentary democracy occurred in Poland.[21] Until this point, and like many of the countries of the former Eastern communist bloc, Poland was unable to fully engage with the ongoing processes of globalisation that were occurring, at different rates, in other parts of the world. Indeed, the collapse of communism left many Eastern European countries in a very poor state both economically and socially.[22] However, at the same time, the end of communism in Poland provided new freedoms that had previously been restricted for citizens of the country; freedoms that included the capacity to migrate beyond national borders. The ability to move into and out of Poland freely would significantly affect migratory patterns in a general sense, but also in football.

From the end of the Second World War to the late-1980s, most Polish footballers were not permitted to make permanent moves outside of the country to ply their athletic labour. During this period, Poland's national team achieved some of its most significant successes, including third place finishes in both the 1974 (Germany) and 1982 (Spain) World Cups, as well as winning an Olympic gold medal in 1972 in Munich and Olympic silvers in 1976 in Montreal (and later in 1992 in Barcelona). During the 1970's, many of Poland's best footballers were playing in Poland. This situation changed, however, at the end of the 1970s when several high-profile Poles were permitted to leave Poland for Europe's more established leagues. These players included Boniek (Juventus), Deyna (Manchester City) and Szarmach (Auxerre).[23] For the most part, however, Poland retained the majority of its most talented players.

After periods of relative strength for Polish football at international level, the period from the mid-1990s to the early 2000s was one of uncertainty, with the national team failing to qualify for any major tournament until the 2002 World Cup Finals. However, whilst the national team struggled, this new democratic period was marked by a move away from Poland's footballing past where leagues were structured around military teams and the police[24] to one where there was an increasing sense of professionalisation, marked by the development of Poland's top league – the Ekstraklasa. The placing of the Ekstraklasa in football's European order has fluctuated in recent years. In UEFA's ranking system, the league has been ranked as high as 17th (in 2001) and as low as 43rd (in 2009). In the latest UEFA ranking, the Ekstraklasa is ranked as the 18th best league in Europe (out of 53). In this respect, it can be argued that the Ekstraklasa sits outside of European football's core economies. This is unsurprising given the manner in which the collapse of communism has impinged the development of football in Eastern European nations.

Whilst the numerical ranking of the Polish Ekstraklasa has fluctuated in recent years, Figure 1 shows how the leagues financial turnover has increased steadily since 2006, rising from 183 m Zloty (41 m Euro) in 2006 to 363 m Zloty (88 m Euro) in 2011.

This increase in turnover might seem to suggest that the league is doing well financially. However, whilst league turnover has shown steady growth in recent

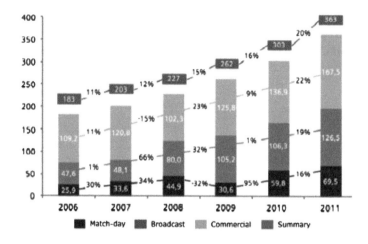

Figure 1.   Ekstraklasa turnover (mln PLN) – 2006/2011.
Source: Deloitte Polska, 2012.

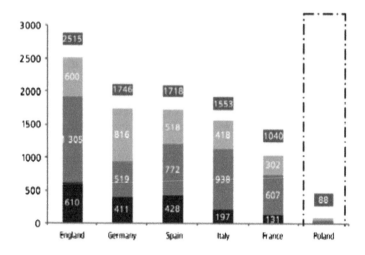

Figure 2.   Turnover of Polish Ekstraklasa relative to Europe's 'big-five' (mln EUR).
Source: Deloitte Polska, 2012.

years, the economic impact of the Ekstraklasa only becomes evident when compared
to Europe's 'big-five'. Then, as Figure 2 shows, it can be seen that the league's
turnover is a fraction of that generated in England, Germany, Spain, Italy and
France.

In this respect, the Ekstraklasa must be positioned alongside leagues with similar
financial profiles. When this is done, and as Figure 3 shows, the Ekstraklasa is
located at the bottom of a group of leagues that includes the Netherlands, Belgium,
Scotland and Austria.

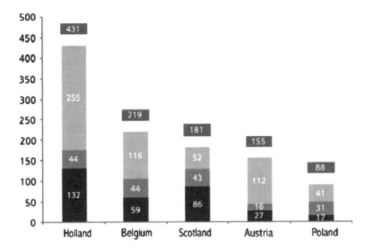

Figure 3. Polish Ekstraklasa turnover grouping (mln EUR).
Source: Deloitte Polska, 2012.

Whilst the Ekstraklasa may not be able to compete financially with some other European leagues, the infrastructural development of the professional game in Poland has been significantly enhanced in recent years leading up to the 2012 UEFA European Championships. The tournament, which was co-hosted by Poland and the Ukraine, resulted in a reported €19b investment being made in Poland's infrastructure.[25] This included major improvements to the country's road and rail networks, and an investment of €2.3b on the renovation of existing stadia and the construction of new facilities. For Poland's football authorities, the hope was that following the tournament, and the significant injection of new investment, a new generation of fans would be attracted to Ekstraklasa matches, thus increasing the income generated from gate receipts and television revenues and enhancing the league's financial status.[26] Beyond the fans, it was also hoped that by hosting European football's showpiece international tournament, Poland's position as a recipient host nation for foreign players could be enhanced. Even before the tournament, this seemed to be a process that was already underway.

The number of foreign players being recruited to the teams of the Ekstraklasa has grown in recent years. For example, whilst only 32 foreign players were playing in the league during the 1998/99 season, 116 were registered with Ekstraklasa teams in 2010/11.[27] In recent years, Ekstraklasa clubs have expanded their scouting networks, and, as a consequence, players from 42 different nations currently play in the league. Of the Ekstraklasa teams, Wisla Krakow and Widzew Lodz have the most multinational squads with players from 15 and 11 different nations represented, respectively.

Of the foreign players represented in the league, the largest numbers originate from Serbia (15), with Slovakia (14) and Brazil (11) following closely behind. In total, there are 77 European players in the league, 19 South Americans, 18 Africans and 2 North Americans.[28] The migratory routes observable in the movements of players into the Ekstraklasa follow similar trends to those observed by Molnar[29] in his examinations of the migrations of professional footballers to Hungary. Like Molnar's analyses, the majority of the Ekstraklasa's migrant players originate from locations with 'geographical proximity, fewer cultural differences, analogous football development and well-functioning agent networks'.[30] In this respect, many of the Ekstraklasa's migrant players originate from other Eastern European nations where similar economic, cultural and political climates exist. This might, in part, explain why some of the migrations occur.

It is clear, however, that migrants playing in the Ekstraklasa also originate from a range of countries located outside of Eastern Europe. For these players, migration to Poland may represent movements to a league more commensurate with the players abilities, or because a lack of opportunity exists in the players home-nation – processes that have been captured in the analyses of athletic movements before.[31] In order to establish if this is the case, a number of foreign players plying their trade in the Ekstraklasa were interviewed. The next part of the paper establishes a framework to capture the motivations of migrant workers moving into the league.

Foreign players in the Ekstraklasa: Method

In order to make some observations with respects to the migrations of foreign players moving into the Polish Ekstraklasa, a qualitative method was employed utilizing individual, semi-structured, face-to-face interviews. Seven migrant players who played in the Ekstraklasa during the 2010/2011 and 2011/2012 seasons were interviewed. As with other studies of this nature,[32] one of the key methodological difficulties lay with access to interviewees – a problem often exacerbated in 'the impregnable world of professional football'.[33] For this study, access was granted via a known gatekeeper based at a Polish Ekstraklasa club. The gatekeeper was able to gain the consent of four migrant players based at the club where he was employed initially, and three further interviews at another Ekstraklasa club that employed him subsequently. All of the players spoke good English and in this regard the decision was taken to conduct the interviews in English for consistency and without the need for translation. All of the interviews were conducted at the clubs in Poland. They were subsequently transcribed in order that a thematic analysis could be conducted to establish the various emergent themes.

For the sake of anonymity, the names of the players have been changed and the teams they play/have played for omitted. The seven players include Oscar, a 30 year old Zimbabwean who has played for three Ekstraklasa clubs over a nine year period; Niko, a 21 year old Croatian international recently purchased from the Croatian Prva HNL league; Aleksander, a 26-year-old Serbian who moved to Poland in 2006; Carlos, a 27–year-old Spaniard who has been playing in the Ekstraklasa since 2007 following a move from the Spanish third division; Aleksy, a 23 year old Hungarian who signed for his Ekstraklasa club in 2012 from a team of the Hungarian Soproni Liga; Filip, a 35-year-old Serbian who is playing for his seventh professional football club in Eastern Europe; and Emmanual, a 24–year-old Gambian player who transferred to the Ekstraklasa in 2012 from a Swedish club. The players were asked a range of questions relating to their motivations to migrate to clubs in the Polish Ekstraklasa, what follows are the responses and an analysis of the findings from the interviews.

Financial rewards

It is apparent that the contemporary professionalization of football has been marked by significant increases in players' salaries, driven, in part, by EU legislation follow-ing the 1995 Bosman ruling, the exponential growth in television revenues and the global expansion strategies pursued by certain leagues and clubs. What is also clear, however, is that not all leagues and teams are able to generate the revenues of Europe's 'big-five' leagues, or clubs such as Manchester United, Barcelona or Bayern Munich. Given the very difficult social and economic position from which Polish professional football has had to develop since the collapse of communism, the Ekstraklasa has clearly not achieved anywhere near the kind of revenue growth observable in Europe's elite leagues, and, as a result, the financial rewards on offer to players in Poland's top division are more limited.

When asked about financial rewards as a motivation to play in Poland, the responses of the players were varied. For example, Niko, when asked if earning a good salary was important, suggested: 'yes, of course it is, it [football] is something where I earn and I live, of course I earn more here than in Croatia'. Aleksander responded in a similar vein: 'we have to be honest, footballers can improve their social situation while playing abroad by earning more money than in homeland domestic leagues'. The Serbian, Filip, felt similarly, however, when asked about earning the best possible salary he also drew attention to various other factors that influenced his decision:

> Of course money is important at this stage of my career. At that time I had offers from other teams as well, but when I came here for tests [club] was playing a home game and when I watched it I decided that I want play at [club]. The atmosphere, fans, city, was very nice so I stayed here. I realized that playing here would be very nice; it would be a pleasure. So the main motive was financial rewards and then opportunity to play at new stadium, with many fans.

The financial rewards available as a professional footballer were significant for the majority of the players interviewed. For the most part, the players suggested that they could command higher salaries in the Ekstraklasa than they could in their home-nation league. Like other spheres of employment, therefore, the ability to take advantage of positive wage disparities would seem to be influential in motivating this group of migrants to select the Ekstraklasa as their migration destination. However, whilst the desires to secure the best possible salary were evident for the players, money alone could not fully capture the complexities of their decisions to migrate.

Playing in Europe's prestigious competitions

It can be argued that the opportunity to play in one of Europe's elite club competi-tions – either the UEFA Champions League or UEFA Europa League – can act as a significant pull factor influencing a migrant player's decision to move to a particular league and, more specifically, particular club.[34] All of the players interviewed for this study were playing at a club where there was an opportunity to play in the qualifying rounds of one of the two competitions; this factor proved to be highly significant in influencing decisions to migrate. Oscar, for example, suggested: 'yeah, that's another thing, [club] is a club which every year they have to play in either the Champions League or the UEFA Cup (Europa League) which is, for every player, a motivation'. Niko echoed Oscar's comment by arguing: 'yes, of course it is, it is motivation'. Niko echoed Oscar's comment by arguing: 'yes, of course it is, it is one of the main reasons, because if a club can play in the Champions League it is one of the main reasons'. Aleksander's response was similar:

> Yes of course I was thinking about it. For every player opportunity of playing in Champions League is something special and something they dream about, so it was one of the reasons.

Carlos reiterated the feelings of the other players, although his interest in playing in a European club competition was linked to securing the best possible playing opportunity, he remarked: 'my motivation was to play in the first league and to try to play in the European Cup'.

Certainly it would seem that the desire to play in one of Europe's elite club competitions, even if only in the qualifying stages, acted as a significant motivating factor for the players interviewed. Indeed, all of the players placed their desire to play in either the UEFA Champions League or the UEFA Europa League very highly when considering their motivations to migrate. However, the desire to play in European competition was related to the broader ambitions of the players and their intention to try and develop their careers as professional footballers.

Ekstraklasa as 'stepping-stone'

It became evident from speaking to the players that they all viewed their time with their Ekstraklasa clubs as being in-flux with aspirations to use the league as a kind of 'stepping-stone' to the bigger Western European leagues. Niko, for example, was very clear about his future intentions:

> I had doubts to maybe wait, maybe another offer would come from another bigger club from Western Europe … but I wanted to keep on my career as soon as possible so I moved here … I think that this is a good station for me to transfer to Western league and it can only go forward … I hope to migrate to Western Europe.

Emmanuel commented in a similar manner and discussed how he felt he could use his time in the Ekstraklasa to move on to a better league elsewhere in Europe. He remarked:

> I took a step when I came here, it feels good to be here, but my next ambition and motivation is to make another step. Of course I want to find out how far can I get. I want to play in a bigger league.

Carlos discussed his move to Poland and the scope for career progression whilst revealing the lack of opportunities he faced in his home-nation. He explained how, in Spain: 'there were five players in the same position … so it was difficult for me to stay and play in Spain'. He went on to add:

> In Spain I was playing in the third league, I didn't have an opportunity to play in the first division and I came here to try to do it. I know it is not the same level, but it can help me to progress in my career … At the beginning I only supposed to stay here for one year, but I decided to sign a longer contract. Now I have two more years and of course I'm happy here, but of course I would like to win a championship in Poland

and then, of course, I would like to improve here or in another country and to try new other leagues.

Carlos and the other players desire to move on from their Ekstraklasa clubs reveal something not only about the players' motivations to select the Ekstraklasa as their migration destination, but also their long-term motivations to improve as athletes and to secure the best possible employment opportunities, wherever they may be located. For Poland's football authorities, it was hoped that hosting the 2012 UEFA European Championships would make the Ekstraklasa a more desirable location for foreign players, providing the very opportunities that the players sought. The players were asked if they thought, within the context of their own careers, this was likely to be the case.

The significance of Euro 2012

Hosting the 14th UEFA European Championships in Poland (and the Ukraine) provided an ideal opportunity not only to make significant investments in the country's football and broader infrastructure, but also to draw attention to the nation as a potential recipient host nation of foreign players. All of the players interviewed had either been playing in Poland before, or had joined Ekstraklasa clubs after, Euro 2012 and, therefore, were asked about the significance of the tournament for football in Poland. When asked if they thought more foreign players would be encouraged to play in Poland following the tournament, the responses were mixed. For example, Emmanuel commented:

> Absolutely. Before Polish people were not used to so many foreigners but now it is changing all the time. I hope I can give other players a motivation that when Polish team come for them they can take it. I think it will change with time.

However, Filip was less convinced that hosting the tournament would encourage more foreign players to play in Poland, as he put it:

> Well it depends what kind of contract offer the players will get. Foreign players must get better deals. They can help with improvement of Ekstraklasa level but only the good players should be hired. I think we can see that many players from Holland or Denmark are coming here, so Poland is very nice option for players. After Euro 2012 Poland have many new stadiums, good fans, so it can help to recruit better players.

Like Filip, Aleksy was unsure about the impact of Euro 2012 on Poland's place as a recipient host nation for foreign players. When asked how he thought hosting the tournament would effect migration to the league, he responded: 'I don't know this. I know Poland has a lot of Polish players, every team has many, and after the Championship maybe more foreign players will come to Poland because this is good league.' However, when asked if he thought that hosting the European Championships had improved football in Poland, he commented:

> No. I think the only thing that improved was infrastructure. The level of Polish football is low. I won't lie, Polish teams are poor, they can't win or even qualify to group stage of Europa League or Champions League. So Ekstraklasa level is very low. Even Polish national team haven't qualified to knockout stage at Euro 2012. I think many things must improve, but I can see huge potential which can be improved.

Foreign players in the Ekstraklasa: Some observations

An analysis of the motivations of migrant professional footballers selecting the Polish Ekstraklasa as their migration destination builds on some of the research already conducted in the area of athletic labour migration. This analysis has shown that migrants are motivated to ply their athletic labour in a foreign country for a number of reasons. With respect to the players examined in this study, the ability to take advantage of positive wage disparities was significant. However, these factors were juxtaposed with the desire to play in European club competitions, and the ambition to further one's career, particularly if the migrant was pushed from their homeland because of a lack of opportunity for career development.

It is somewhat unsurprising that the migrants examined in this analysis did not place a greater emphasis on financial reward. This is not to say that salary was insignificant – on the contrary – the need to make ends meet was clearly important. Important also was the capacity to be able to take advantage of the positive wage disparities that existed between the Ekstraklasa and the migrants' home-nation leagues. However, all responses relating to contract and salary seemed to come with the realization that the Ekstraklasa is not one of European football's elite leagues and on this basis, whilst money was important, it was always felt that other factors were more important; factors such as playing in Europe's elite club competitions.

The players interviewed placed great value on the desire to play in either the UEFA Champions League or UEFA Europa League – even if only in the qualifying rounds. It would seem that this desire stemmed from their competitive nature whereby the players sought to prove themselves at the highest levels and against the best competition. Playing in these competitions was also important though because the players felt that these competitions could act as a kind of 'shop-window' through which they could be spotted, increasing the likelihood of being scouted by a bigger club in a more established European league. Combined, both elements showed that ambition clearly comprized a significant component of the decision to migrate.

All of the players interviewed expressed a desire to move on from the Ekstraklasa to one of Europe's more established leagues. In this respect, it was clear that the migrants saw the league as a 'stepping-stone' in their careers. Whether or not the league can actually provide such a function is beyond the scope of this analysis. However, given that three of the players interviewed had already spent a significant period of their career in the league, it might seem unlikely that time spent in the Ekstraklasa has prepared these players for upward-migrations to more established leagues. This does not mean, though, that the Ekstraklasa is not a desirable migration destination for certain types of migrants.

Arguably, the Eastern European players interviewed had selected the Ekstraklasa because it represented the highest quality league commensurate with their abilities, but, importantly, also a league that they could move to with relative ease, given the geographical proximity of the country and the social, economic and cultural similarities – pull factors already identified as important in the migrations of Eastern European players by Molnar and Maguire[35] in their study of Hungarian football, and in other sports.[36]

For the players who originated from outside of Eastern Europe, the social and cultural pull factors were of less significance. In these cases, it was push factors that were more prominent, specifically the lack of opportunity in the athletes' home-nation, which, for these players occurred in two different ways. For the

African players, the lack of opportunity for career development in Zimbabwe and Gambia exists because of the limited number of professional playing opportunities in those countries; a problem that exists for many African players of greater ability, many of whom now migrate to Europe to ply their trade.[37] Therefore, these players may have been pushed from Africa to Europe where many more opportunities to secure a professional career in the game exist. Whilst the Ekstraklasa might exist on the periphery of Europe's football economy, a move to this league still represents advancement for these players. For the player from Spain, the problem was somewhat different.

Originating from a nation that sits at the economic core of the game, possesses one of Europe's 'big-five' leagues and whose national team are recent World and European Champions, there is clearly not a lack of professional playing opportunities in Spain. However, what there may be is an overproduction of indigenous athletic talent, a level of competition which is simply too great for some players and a league which provides both the salary and the desirability to attract some of the world's most talented foreign players. These sorts of problems have been identified in research before.[38] When these factors are combined, they push those athletes who are unable to secure playing opportunities in their home-nation out to various other leagues – in this case, the Polish Ekstraklasa. Whilst the player interviewed for this study could continue playing in Spain, this was in the country's third division. In Poland, the player has the opportunity to play in the first division, and also European competition, opportunities that would not be available in Spain and which underline both the importance of ambition in structuring migration motives, but also the manner in which some migrants are required to locate the best employment opportunities outside of their home-nation.

For Poland's football authorities, hosting the 2012 European Championships provided an ideal opportunity to develop both the infrustructural conditions and profile of the game in the country, thus, potentially improving, and to a point, marketing, the employment opportunities available in the Ekstraklasa. Whilst the players' perceptions of improvements following the tournament were mixed, references were made to increased numbers of fans and improved stadia in interviews. It is obviously too early to say exactly how beneficial hosting the tournament might be for Polish football. However, these early indicators suggest that Poland may become a more desirable host nation for foreign players in the near future, if current upward trends in foreign player numbers, combined with increased attendances and stadia development, are considered.

Conclusion

This analysis has identified that the Polish Ekstraklasa is not one of Europe's elite football leagues. Indeed, whilst revenues are continuing to grow in the league, its turnover still places it amongst a group that mostly comprises Europe's middle-order leagues. This is somewhat unsurprising given that the development of professional football in Poland is reflective of a series of challenges left over from the legacy of the communist regime. Unlike Western European leagues that have developed over decades in capitalist, and increasingly, globalized and mediatized economies, the development of the Ekstraklasa has been hindered not only by the loss of state funding and a range of other geopolitical and economic challenges, but also simply because other leagues in Western Europe have been able, in the interim period, to establish themselves in the European football system. The result is that the Polish Ekstraklasa now finds itself in a state of 'dependent-development' based largely on the limited financial resources of the Ekstraklasa clubs relative to the teams of the more established Western European leagues. Because the league finds itself in this position, the most talented indigenous players will usually seek employment outside of Poland in one of the more established European leagues (although it should be noted that these players are few in number relative to other talent exporting countries). Meanwhile, the Ekstraklasa clubs are left to recruit those indigenous players who either cannot or do not want to migrate from Poland and migrants, such as those examined in this paper, who are unable, for one reason or another, to secure employment in the more prestigious European leagues and who, in some cases, may have been pushed from their home-nation.

Whilst the development of the Ekstraklasa has been slower relative to other leagues in Western Europe and the numbers of foreign players plying their trade in the league is still relatively small compared to some of Europe's more established leagues, it would appear that the Ekstraklasa still has much to offer migrants who might not be able to secure employment in one of football's core economies. Firstly, and irrespective of the leagues financial development, migration to the Ekstraklasa still provides an opportunity for players to secure greater financial rewards than may be available in other leagues such as those located in Africa or in other Eastern European nations. Secondly, the Ekstraklasa provides an opportunity for migrants to play in a top division when this opportunity might be limited elsewhere. Thirdly, migrants playing in one of the leagues' top teams may have the opportunity to play in the qualifying rounds of one of Europe's elite club competitions, thus showcasing their talents at higher levels and to bigger audiences. Fourthly, it may be possible that the Ekstraklasa can be used as a stepping-stone to a more established league in Western Europe (although the evidence to support this argument is limited from this analysis).

Clearly, a series of pull factors are at work that motivates migrants to select the Polish Ekstraklasa as their migration destination. However, rarely will these pull factors work in isolation. More commonly they will work in tandem with a series of push factors that will propel migrants from particular locations. In this respect, whilst the more personal benefits of a move to Poland, such as financial reward, or the opportunity to play in the UEFA Champions League or UEFA Europa League should be considered to be important, significant also are factors such as the lack of opportunity for career development in an athlete's home-nation, or the overproduction of athletic talent in certain places. Arguably, both the pull and push factors were at work for the migrants examined in this study.

It is still too early to say whether or not hosting the 2012 UEFA European Championships will have any lasting effect on the development of the Ekstraklasa and professional football in Poland more broadly. It would certainly appear that a significant amount of investment has been made into stadia, training facilities and broader infrastructure as part of the hosting. Whilst some migrant players may choose to use the Ekstraklasa as a 'shop-window' through which they can be spotted, arguably both Poland and the Ukraine have had an opportunity to showcase their countries and facilities to players from all over Europe and the world more broadly, via the media attention that was focused on the two nations for the duration of the tournament. If the continued development of football in these nations is managed effectively, the 2012 UEFA European Championships could represent a watershed moment for Polish football and sport in Eastern Europe more broadly.

Notes

1. Baade and Metheson, *Mega Sporting Events in Developing Nations*.
2. Deloitte, *Annual Review of Football Finance*.
3. Elliott and Weedon, *Feet-Drain or Feet-Exchange*.
4. Magee and Sugden, *The World at Their Feet*.
5. See Bohning; Fischer et al., Magee and Sugden.
6. Taylor, *Global players?*
7. See Poli et al.
8. See Deloitte, *Annual Review of Football Finance*.
9. Taylor, *Global players?*
10. See, e.g. *The annually Produced Deloitte Review of Football Finance*; *Football Money League*.
11. Andreff, 'The Economic Effects of Muscle-Drain in Sport'.
12. Fischer et al., 'Interdependencies Between Development and Migration'.
13. Maguire and Pearton, *The Impact of Elite Labour Migration on the Identification, Selection and Development of European Soccer Players*, 761.
14. See Maguire and Stead; Molnar and Maguire; Stead and Maguire.
15. Magee and Sugden, *The World at Their Feet*.
16. Carter, *In Foreign Fields*, 5.
17. Magee and Sugden, *The World at Their Feet*.
18. See Elliott and Maguire, 2008a, 2008b, 2011; Maguire 1988, 1996.
19. Elliott and Harris, *Crossing the Atlantic*.
20. Darby, *Out of Africa*; Darby et al., *Football Academies and the Migration of African Football Labour to Europe*.
21. Prazmowska, *A History of Poland*.
22. See Molnar, *Hungarian Football: A Socio-Historical Perspective*.
23. Lanfranchi and Taylor, *Moving with the Ball*.
24. Lenartowisz and Karwacki, *An Overview of Social Conflicts in the History of Polish Club Football*.
25. Cienski and Olearchyk, 'Euro 2012 to Leave a More Valuable Legacy'.
26. Deloiite Polska.
27. Stec, 'Ekstraklasa More and More Foreign'.
28. Stec, 'Ekstraklasa More and More Foreign'.
29. Molnar, *Mapping Migrations: Hungary Related Migrations of Professional Footballers After the Collapse of Communism*; 'From the Soviet Bloc to the European Community'.
30. Molnar, *Mapping Migrations: Hungary Related Migrations of Professional Footballers After the Collapse of Communism*, 468.
31. See Elliott and Maguire, 2008b; Elliott and Harris, 2011; Maguire, 1996.
32. See Magee and Sugden, *The World at Their Feet*, for example.
33. Magee and Sudgen, *The World at Their Feet*, 423.
34. See Lanfranchi and Taylor, 2001; Magee and Sugden, 2002.
35. Molnar and Maguire, *Hungarian Footballers on the Move*.
36. See Elliott and Maguire, 2008b; Genest, 1994; Maguire, 1996.
37. Darby et al., *Football Academies and the Migration of African Football Labour to Europe*.
38. See Elliott and Maguire, 2008b; Elliott and Harris, 2011; Miller et al., 2003.

References

Andreff, Wladimir. 'The Economic Effect of 'Muscle-Drain' in Sport'. In *Labour Market Migration in European Football: Issues and Challenges*, eds. Geoff Walters, and Giambattista Rossi, 9–31. London: Birkbeck Sports Business Centre, 2009.

Baade, Robert, and Victor Matheson. 'Mega-Sporting Events in Developing Nations: Playing the Way to Prosperity'. *South African Journal of Economics* 72 (2004): 1085–103.

Bohning, Wolf. *Studies in International Labour Migration*. Basingstoke: Macmillan, 1984.

Carter, Thomas. *In Foreign Fields: The Politics and Experiences of Transnational Sport Migration*. London: Pluto, 2011.

Cienski, Jan, and Roman Olearchyk. 'Euro 2012 to Leave a More Valuable Legacy'. *Financial Times*, June 14, 2012.

Darby, Paul. 'Out of Africa: The Exodus of African Football Talent to Europe'. *Working USA: The Journal of Labour and Society* 10, no. 4 (2007): 443–56.

Darby, Paul, Gerard Akindes, and Matthew Kirwin. 'Football Academies and the Migration of African Football Labour to Europe'. *Journal of Sport and Social Issues* 31, no. 2 (2007): 143–61.

Deloitte. *Annual Review of Football Finance*. Manchester: Deloitte, 2011.

Deloitte Polska. *Football League Finance for 2010: The Position in Europe*. Deloitte Polska: Poland, 2012.

Elliott, Richard, and John Harris. 'Crossing the Atlantic from Football to Soccer: Preliminary Observations on the Migrations of English Players and the Internationalization of Major League Soccer'. *Working USA: The Journal of Labour and Society* 14, no. 4 (2011): 555–68.

Elliott, Richard, and Joseph Maguire. 'Getting Caught in the Net': Examining the Recruitment of Canadian Players in British Professional Ice Hockey'. *Journal of Sport and Social Issues* 32, no. 2 (2008a): 158–76.

Elliott, Richard, and Joseph Maguire. 'Thinking Outside of the Box': Exploring a Conceptual Synthesis for Research in the Area of Athletic Labour Migration'. *Sociology of Sport Journal* 25, no. 4 (2008b): 482–97.

Elliott, Richard, and Joseph Maguire. "Net-Gains': Informal recruiting, Canadian Players and British Professional Ice Hockey'. In *Sport and Migration: Borders, boundaries and crossings*, eds. Joseph Maguire and Mark Falcous, 102–11. London: Routledge, 2011.

Elliott, Richard, and Gavin Weedon. 'Foreign Players in the Premier Academy League: 'Feet-Drain' or 'Feet-Exchange'?' *International Review for the Sociology of Sport* 46, no. 1 (2010): 61–75.

Fischer, Peter, Martin Reiner, and Thomas Straubhaar. 'Interdependencies Between Development and Migration'. In *International Migration, Immobility and Development: Multidisciplinary Perspectives*, eds. Tomas Hammar, Grete Brochmann, Kristof Tamas and Thomas Faist, 91–132. Oxford: Berg, 1997.

Genest, Simon. 'Skating on Thin Ice? The International Migration of Canadian Ice Hockey Players'. In *The Global Sports Arena: Athletic Talent Migration in an Interdependent World*, eds. John Bale and Joseph Maguire, 112–25. London: Frank Cass, 1994.

Joseph, Maguire. 'Blade Runners: Canadian Migrants, Ice Hockey and the Global Sports Process'. *Journal of Sport and Social Issues* 21, no. 3 (1996): 335–60.

Lanfranchi, Pierre, and Matthew Taylor. *Moving with the Ball: The Migration of Professional Footballers*. Oxford: Berg, 2001.

Lenartowisz, Michal, and Adam Karwacki. 'An Overview of Social Conflicts in the History of Polish Club Football'. *European Journal for Sport and Society* 2, no. 2 (2005): 97–107.

Magee, John, and John Sugden. '"The World at Their Feet": Professional Football and International Labour Migration'. *Journal of Sport and Social Issues* 26, no. 4 (2002): 421–37.

Maguire, Joseph. 'The Commercialization of English Elite Basketball 1972-1988: A Figurational Perspective'. *International Review for the Sociology of Sport* 23, no. 4 (1988): 305–22.

Maguire, Joseph, Grant Jarvie, Louise Mansfield, and Joe Bradley. *Sport Worlds: A Sociological Perspective*. Champaign: Human Kinetics, 2002.

Maguire, Joseph, and Robert Pearton. 'The Impact of Elite Labour Migration on the Identification, Selection and Development of European Soccer Players'. *Journal of Sports Sciences* 18 (2000): 759–69.

Maguire, Joseph, and David Stead. 'Border Crossings: Soccer Labour Migration and the European Union'. *International Review for the Sociology of Sport* 33, no. 1 (1998): 59–73.

Miller, Toby, David Rowe, Jim McKay, and Gary Lawrence. 'The Over-Production of US Sports and the New International Division of Cultural Labour'. *International Review for the Sociology of Sport* 38, no. 4 (2003): 427–40.

Molnar, Gyozo. 'Mapping Migrations: Hungary-Related Migrations of Professional Footballers After the Collapse of Communism'. *Soccer and Society* 7, no. 4 (2006): 463–85.

Molnar, Gyozo. 'Hungarian Football: A Socio-Historical Perspective'. *Sport in History* 27, no. 2 (2007): 293–318.

Molnar, Gyozo, and Joseph Maguire. 'Hungarian Footballers on the Move: Issues and Observations on the First Migratory Phase'. *Sport in Society* 11, no. 1 (2008): 74–89.

Molnar, Gyozo. 'From the Soviet Bloc to the European Community: Migrating Professional Footballers into and Out of Hungary'. In *Sport and Migration: Borders, Boundaries and Crossings*, eds. Joseph Maguire and Mark Falcous, 56–70. London: Routledge, 2011.

Poli, Rafaelle, Loic Ravenel, and Roger Besson. *Annual Review of the European Football Players' Labour Market*. Neuchatel: Professional Football Players Observatory, 2011.

Prazmowska, Anita. *A History of Poland*. Basingstoke: Palgrave Macmillan, 2004.

Stead, David, and Joseph Maguire. '"Rite de Passage or Passage to Riches?": The Motivation and Objectives of Nordic/Scandinavian Players in English League Soccer'. *Journal of Sport and Social Issues* 24, no. 1 (2000): 36–60.

Stec, Rafal. *Ekstraklasa More and More Foreign: Poland not for Poles*. http://www.Sport.pl (accessed January 23, 2012) 2010.

Taylor, Matthew. 'Global Players? Football, Migration and Globalisation: 1930–2000'. *Historical Social Research* 31, no. 1 (2006): 7–30.

"Sometimes you go into competitions with little or no expectations": England, Euro 2012 in the context of austerity

Peter Kennedy

Department of Social Science, Media and Journalism, Glasgow Caledonian University, Glasgow, Scotland

This paper analyses media coverage of the England football team in the run up to Euro 2012. The study also describes the dominant discourse of 'low expectations' underpinning media representations of England and considers various reasons for this. Short-term factors are considered, including the resignation of the England manager, the intra-team tensions arising from racism, along with longer-term factors, including the perceived constraints placed on the England national team's development by the English Premier League. While these factors are important, they cannot alone, or even in combination, sufficiently explain why the discourse of 'low expectations took such a hold over media representations of the England national team. One missing factor is the broader problems facing the economy and society, particularly the preoccupation with 'austerity', which has created an aura of low expectations; particularly, the tendency to represent 'austerity' *as* 'growth' in a 'low expectations' culture. Previous research has demonstrated the links between the fortunes of the wider economy and sentiments surrounding the fate of the English national team. This article takes the opportunity to reconsider these wider links in terms of an *elective affinity*, arguing that the discourse of 'low expectations' haunting the England team in the present period is the manifestation and transference of a more pervasive general lowering of expectations among the media and the political elite, concerning the present and future political economic prospects of economic growth and social prosperity.

Introduction

Media coverage of the England football team at the Euro 2012 football championships held in June converged around a discourse of 'low expectations'. The discourse, as will be shown, has different sub-plots, including, to manage downward expectations to circumvent media criticism of poor performances, as psychological relief to players, or as a means of transforming judgements about England at the Euros from 'finals' to mere transitory 'preparations' for future tournaments, etc. Although this article's main objective is to explore some of these sub-plots, the other aim of the article is to examine the context for this discourse in broader structural dilemmas and concerns within society, particularly linked to political, social and economic changes occurring in the UK that have their origins in the global economy. To establish the basis of the textual analysis, this introduction sets the scene with a preliminary overview of the wider political economic context, as it relates to elite professional English football.

In England, the material and ideological links between football and the wider political economy have become more clearly defined since the emergence of the English Premier League (EPL) two decades ago. The EPL has established a clear business ethic for its members, which ensures clubs are increasingly commercial in scope and practice as a result. Indeed, the EPL is expressive of a wider political economy, shaped by neo-liberal beliefs about the economic efficiencies and inherently democratic values inscribed in lightly regulated markets and private ownership. In more fundamental terms, football operates in a context where the emphasis on the market, the private sector and a more entrepreneurial state have served to reorder public and civil institutions in ways that *sharpen the conflict between use value and exchange value* as the determining factor in the production of civic sector, public sector and cultural sector goods and services as commodities first and foremost.[1] This conflict, formerly disguised by the language of 'stake-holding partnerships' by 'third way' proponents[2] and represented as a technical choice based on 'what works', arises from a more deeply ingrained social relationship – the *commodity form,* which is inherent to market capitalist economies ('free' or otherwise) and manifest in the *social* (i.e. not technical) binary, public versus market interests.[3] In relation to football, this social binary – public versus market interests – operates at two levels: a) between clubs and national team and b) between elite football per se and the wider political economy.

The social binary between the English national team's development and the EPL manifests in the possible conflict of interests between public good vis-a-vis the commercial interests and money motivated aspirations dominating clubs within the EPL.[4] For example, the England team may prove unable to live up to the role of 'public good' in the eyes of fans and the media (as an expression of national pride, non-market identities, etc.) due to the (increasingly insurmountable) limits placed on it by the commercial imperatives of the EPL (itself an outgrowth of neo-liberal enterprise in sport). While national team success does have commercial consequences (the financial viability of the English Football Association relies on this), the aspiration to achieve national success is largely a non-commercial use value manifest in the forging of national identities and patriotic fervour. Of course, use values can be *ab*used (for example, through the attempted assimilation of social group interests into specific ideologies concerning 'the national interest'). The point is, however, that whatever kind of use value national sides signify, it comes up against the formidable force of the exchange value, profit motivated interests of the EPL. The recent deal struck by SKY and BT worth a combined £3.5 billion over the next four years, would appear to offer further confirmation that the 'Premier League product' is here to stay for the foreseeable future:[5] The consequences of the latter are taken up in more detail later.

The above social binary between the England national team and the EPL also has its context within the social binary *between football and the wider political economy.* In both cases, the relation is one of *elective affinity* rather than 'superstructure' mapping perfectly on to 'base'.[6] Both the fortunes of the EPL and of English media preoccupation with expectations about a 'golden generation' of English players conquering world football, have arisen within a wider neo-liberal political economy prioritising financialization of production and consumption, speculative short-term decision-making, a narrow economistic view of success and a pathological intolerance for long-term investments for future development. Moreover, the same neo-liberalism also tends to promote patholog-ical exuberance, unrealistically high expectations. In the wider political economy, this revolves around the pathologies of 'growth' financed by debt. In national football, it became manifest in unsubstantiated (speculative) exuberance about the fortunes of the England national football team and the 'world class' quality of England players. The fact that, for the present at least, the EPL has contin-ued to thrive in times of economic crises (a relatively safe haven for surplus capital), while the UK economy is now beset by a discourse of low expecta-tions, presents a double negative for the English national team. On the one hand, it is more securely caught in the slipstream of an EPL consolidating its place in the football landscape. On the other hand (as I go on to detail below), sentiments surrounding the England team become increasingly infected by wider, much more negative sentiments surrounding the fate of neo-liberalism at the level of the wider political economy.

This study aims to explore how the above social binaries lie at the heart of the narrative of 'low expectations' dominating media reportage of the England team in the run up to and during Euro 2012. The paper begins by outlining the extent to which a discourse of 'low expectations' dominated media representations and the particular sub-plots of its domination and then considers a number of salient reasons for this discourse, before centring on the influence of discourses operating in the wider political economy related to the economic crisis and how this is being played out in the UK. It is suggested that an elective affinity exists between media discourse on the national football team and the wider economy. This elective affinity becomes observable in the contrary aspirations of national team and EPL. In this sense the discourse of 'low expectations', so pronounced in media representations, arises from both the wider economic context *and* the inter-mediate context between nation and club.

When examining the dialectic between media text and wider context, data were collected from a careful examination of over 100 media articles situated in the sports section of national newspapers and online sites dedicated to football reportage; in addition to an examination of the TV commentary produced by both the BBC and ITV. The chosen time period for considering the data spanned the month leading up to Euro 2012 until the week after England exited the tournament, roughly from the beginning of May until the end of June 2012. As one might expect, the period revealed shifts in the pre-tournament discourse and its subsequent development at key points during the tournament, in particular the build up to the first game, the aftermath of the first game and England's exit from the tournament. Letters pages and fan forums were not analysed because these data are by definition overwhelm-ingly from supporters when the central purpose of this research is on media and not fan representations.

As intimated above when referring to the dialectic between 'text' and 'context', the theoretical orientation of the paper is shaped by the view that language, words, or more precisely discourses, are active ingredients in shaping social practice, shaping what is known as well as the knower. From such a perspective, keywords are nodes around which ideological battles are fought. They are entry points into a wider analysis,[7] offering a framework for organizing the meaning of texts.[8] As also intimated, the paper is shaped by the view that the dialectic between text and context has the extra discursive vitality of the commodity form of capitalist production and the various ways this form manifests itself (currently neo-liberal) as its basis.

The paper also accepts advice that authors ought to be clear about their own value orientation[9] because discourse is,

> A social practice ... implying a dialectical relationship between people and groups of people. It is constitutive both in the sense that it helps to sustain and reproduce the status quo, and in the sense that it contributes to transforming it.[10]

In this respect, it is the extra-discursive realm of commodity production and the author's critical standpoint towards it, which informs the value orientation of this paper.

The narrative of 'low expectations'

At the beginning of this paper, it was suggested that media coverage of the England football team at the Euro 2012 football championships held in June converged around a discourse of 'low expectations'. It was also suggested that different sub-plots, including, to manage downward expectations, to circumvent media criticism of poor performances, as psychological relief to players, or as a means of transforming judgements about England at the Euros from 'finals' to mere transitory 'preparations' for future tournaments. This discourse, which we explore below in more detail, is in complete contrast to recent decades. Prior to Euro 2012, England football teams usually enter the final stages of an international tournament with an adrenalin rush fuelled by national hopes and media hypes full of aspirations of conquering the world of football,

> Entering the 2006 World Cup on the back of two successive quarter-final finishes at the 2002 World Cup and the 2004 European Championships, optimism radiated that this time England could win the World Cup. Set against this high level of expectation several newspapers drew on one of England's favourite invented historical traditions, Admiral Horatio Nelson's famous message to the British fleet, from his flagship HMS Victory, before the Battle of Trafalgar was about to start.[11]

Of course, recent decades also reveal how hope and glory soon turn sour. When the England team inevitably exit the tournament much earlier than expectations would have us believe possible, then, following trend, hype turns to despair as the would-be conquerors of the world became *post hoc* zeros, who,

> Got what they deserved – absolutely nichts. Complacent to the last, Eriksson and his spoilt players failed to achieve the momentum that better sides have displayed.[12]

Perhaps more mindful of the hype of old, but also of the changing economic environment too, *The Economist* offered a more hard-headed and contextualized judgment on the England team prior to the World Cup finals in South Africa in 2010:

> As this [2010] World Cup begins, think back to the last one, in 2006. Britain was still enjoying an economic boom that, to many, seemed set to last forever. The housing market and the FTSE were rising, apparently inexorably. People borrowed too much to buy their houses, then borrowed more for cars and holidays. The government was just as profligate. In retrospect it is clear the country was living in a bubble of hubris and unearned kudos ...

> The England football team exemplified this collective delusion, and the country's rampant materialism … The team itself was feted as a 'golden generation' of English footballers. It was expected – almost, it seemed, entitled – to win the cup. Alas, as with the economy, the commentators had mistaken swagger for authentic talent.[13]

The Economist reveals a degree of prescience not usually found in the mainstream media of the time, concerning the relationship between the fortunes of the economy and national sentiments about the England team. However, this was 2010 and although the economy was contracting the full effects of this contraction on national sentiment per se had still not surfaced (public sector cuts were still under discussion, still at the stage of announcements, rather than actual). The tendency was for media representations followed trend with respect to the fortunes of the England team: immense highs followed by troughs of despair. Hence, for the most part, the debacle and soul-searching following England's exit in 2006 is forgotten, as 'we' are (once again) reassured that England ought to be considered one of the world top four rankings,

> … several experts reckoned the English side, managed by Fabio Capello, could make the final four, only a handful felt they would reach the final itself or lift the famous trophy.[14]

The optimism is short lived and despair set in as England crashed out of the 2010 tournament. If one were to invent a media 'hypergraph' charting England's hopes and despairs between 2002–2010, it would depict a magnitude of boom and slump bordering on the pathological.

However, since 2010 our imaginary graph, if not exactly 'flat-lined', has become subdued. Those wild oscillations, so much a feature of previous tournaments for the best part of two decades, were markedly absent from media reportage of the England football team's progress prior to and during Euro 2012. For example, on the eve of the tournament (when previously most of the hype is at its most 'hyper-hopeful'), the media was uncharacteristically muted about the England team's prospects:

> There have been no questions as to whether England can win the entire competition. There has been no columns asserting that not only can England win the whole competition but can do so without conceding a single goal. There has been no radio commentaries suggesting that not only can England win the competition, while conceding no goals, but can do so even if they field the surviving members of the team that won the 1966 World Cup.[15]

Indeed, a casual web search of the term 'low expectations' and 'England football team', brings forth an avalanche of low expectations discourse, operating in and through a number of motivating sub-plots, including *to keep up hopes, to create conditions for success* (for example, 'hopefully we can go under the radar until the latter stages of the tournament and get further than we have done before';[16] *as a reaction to the previous misguided optimism* (for example, 'after optimism fails, England fans try low expectations');[17] *to boost team morale, or to manage media expectations* (for example, 'If Hodgson's dedication to the ploy is firm, then failure must be made a theme of England's preparation');[18] *as manager strategy* (for example, 'by taking charge of a side that, for once, no-one in the normally hysterical English media expects to do well, might just work in his favour. With the pressure off, he might get England to do better than they usually do in major tournaments')[19]; or *to create collective team ethic* (for example, 'England's most talented team but on the evidence of its first performance against France, it is a team in which every individual knows his role and is willing to give everything for team and country).[20]

The narrative of 'low expectations' encodes the management of what is meant by 'success' in a changed environment:

> No new manager, least of all a new England manager, would choose to come into the job and begin to lower everyone's expectations, though in Hodgson's defence he is merely continuing a process begun by woeful displays under Fabio Capello and Steve McClaren. Capello in particular seemed to be haunted by the ineptitude he had to answer for at the last World Cup, and Hodgson shrewdly appears to have realised that with that level of performance as a base, the only way is up.[21]

According to this narrative, Roy Hodgson's appointment is seen as part of a discursive strategy to lower expectations concerning England's performance. The implication is that there is an alternative reason why, one time favourite, Harry Redknapp had not been chosen on grounds other than his perceived 'suitability' for the post, which is that his natural optimism may have run against the grain of the prevailing narrative of low expectations. The phrase, 'Hodgson shrewdly', moreover, seems to suggest, on the part of the media, that Hodgson has some awareness of this. In the FA press conference announcing Hodgson's appointment as England team coach, Hodgson reflects:

> England has always got to go into tournaments thinking they can win. It's going to be a little bit more difficult on this occasion because the man who qualified the team has left the team and I have had to take over at a fairly late stage, but I certainly think the players would be disappointed if we thought anything less from them than an attempt to win the tournament and it is very important ... everyone gets behind the team ... All we can do in the coming years ahead, in the Euros and beyond is to give England the best footballing team that we have been hoping for since 1966.[22]

Here, Hodgson is careful not to state he expects England to win the tournament. Instead he states that the players would be disappointed if the nation thought they were incapable of competing on this stage, though crucially his comment also deflects tournament success from Euro 2012 to some point in the future. Of course, it is also likely that compensation and contractual issues, along with Hodgson's international experiences and clear intention to embrace the entire English coaching set up rather than preoccupation with the first team, played a part in his appointment.[23] Nevertheless, the discourse around Hodgson's appointment can clearly be seen as a departure from the grand expectations of the previous decades, and more embracive of the narrative of 'low expectations':

> The FA admires Hodgson's tournament experience and his standing within Uefa and Fifa, but his primary role will be to get the best from the senior team.[24]

> The new manager has not been set any 'fixed minimum target' but it is hoped he will take England to the 2014 World Cup finals in Brazil and the 2016 European Championship in France.[25]

Here, the rhetoric of 'Getting the best from senior players' and the hope of qualification for tournament finals would seem to be a far cry from the rhetoric of potential world-beaters in waiting. This realism was also fully embraced by the players prior to the tournament:

> It would be stupid of me to set any goals or targets. Of course, everyone's dream is to win a tournament but it would be stupid to set that as a target. There have been teams in the past that have won this tournament who haven't necessarily been favourites so we have to go there and do as well as we can. (Stephen Gerrard)

> The most important thing is if we go out there ... and perform well and work hard as a team, put in 100% for the fans that travel. That's all that we can ask for. (Theo Walcott)

Nevertheless, it would appear that, under the unspoken motto: expect the worst, hope for the best, the narrative of 'low expectations' repositions the 'lame duck' in a more positive light as the valiant 'underdog', who, freed from the burden of expectation, might prove naysayers wrong, not by winning the tournament, but simply giving their opposition 'a good game'.

The upside of this downbeat message is that it could potentially help England 'sneak up' on its opponents, catch them off guard and deliver some unlikely 'success'; sentiments echoed by a number of BBC Sport pundits and ex-footballers:

> I don't see many people actually saying, 'we can win this tournament', whereas in previous tournaments there's been huge pressure placed on them at all, so that might play to their advantage. (Alan Shearer)

> It is the first time I can remember when everybody is playing them down, normally everybody is saying we can do this, or we can win, or get to the semi-final, and I think this time around everyone is kind of thinking, I don't think our chances are very good: I think that is very good for England ... sometimes you go into competitions with little or no expectations and things happen for you ... I think that is what will happen to England in the tournament. (Mark Lawrenson)[26]

The above evidence is part of the more abundant evidence in the media concerning the pervasiveness of the narrative of low expectations regarding the England team's fate at Euro 2012. As mentioned, this narrative lies in stark contrast to the narratives of hope and despair, which tended to saturate previous media coverage of the England team during major international championships. The next section of this paper attempts to explain reasons underpinning this stark contrast in media representation.

Explaining the narrative of 'low expectations'

To some extent, the narrative of low expectations is part consequence of previous reactions to emotional booms and busts with respect to England's fate in past tournament competition. It is also the product of the fall in status accorded English football in the years proceeding Euro 2012, due to a number of important inter-related factors. The sudden resignation of Fabio Capello, the England team coach (already a source of derision and disillusion), is one such factor. Despite the sports media's evident disenchantment with Capello's style of management, he oversaw

England to the top of their qualifying group, taking 18 points from a possible 24 on the back of impressive wins away from home against Switzerland and Bulgaria. Capello's sudden departure put what had been achieved in qualification in jeopardy. Alongside this factor, there were also fears that the small core of players, once described as the 'golden generation', had passed their prime and that as a consequence England would be found wanting in the final stages of Euro 2012: as Neville (prior to becoming assistant England coach!) outlined, 'I'm not having a go at individuals; there are some very good players among those names. Collectively, Rooney aside, there is hardly any pace, very little invention and hardly any rotation of positions'.[27] If the situation of the golden generation being past its peak, the sacking of Capello and general lack of faith in the calibre of the England team were not enough, the situation, it was argued, was further compounded by the shame of racial slurs and counter-slurs among players at the highest level in the full glare of the media, as the escalating row between John Terry and Rio Ferdinand threatened to 'fracture the England dressing room'.[28]

Each of the above reasons has their place in any explanation. However, perhaps a more serious obstacle of a more enduring nature is the barrier the EPL places in the way of progress for the national team. Initial claims made by the new EPL in 1992 that the breakaway EPL would inspire football excellence and a slimmed down league that would benefit the national team, have not materialized. On the contrary, since its inception in 1992, the EPL has encouraged the inflow of capital, while the Bosman ruling has only served to accelerate the international flow of players and inflation of elite salaries, which lock clubs into over-spend and mounting debt. Moreover, the financial necessity to stay in the EPL (relegated clubs can lose up to £38 million) takes increasing preference over all decision-making, to the degree that,

> The demand for quick success from trigger-happy chairmen ensures that the state of the national team is placed at the bottom of any agenda for the managers, just after AOB[29] ... In the relentless drive to keep TV companies and audiences around the world happy, how much importance will club chairmen place on recruiting young English talent with all that money for foreign superstars burning a hole in their pockets?[30]

The result, for some, is that the EPL's neo-liberal regime exerts a negative impact on youth development and coaching styles at club level, the pool from which the England national team is recruited,

> ... the Premier League has failed to develop a strong English coaching culture, relying at the top on European coaches and Ferguson, a Scot.[31]

The more developed claim would appear to be that players in the current youth setup in England, which forms the basis of the pyramid from which elite footballers are eventually drawn, are coached for too long without the ball and placed in competitive teams playing on full size pitches – where the overriding concern is winning matches instead of experimenting with the ball – far too early in their development. Put another way, the neo-liberal regime consigns youth to the status of proto-commodities. As part of a feeder system to top clubs, it is not so much guaranteed time on the pitch but to be 'match ready' and those who cannot endure this regime are easily and quickly discarded (into the lower reaches of the English leagues, mainly). Treat youth as commodities (runs the argument) and they may behave in similar fashion by becoming their own private corporations marketing their own brands to the highest bidder, with an increasing eye towards their consumer status and celebrity image rights.

Whatever the accuracy of the above – a discourse linking the EPL to the fate of the English team – there has been little headway in tackling the EPL model and the situation would appear to be one of consolidation: the grip of the EPL model over English football has recently been strengthened to the sum of £3 billion as a result of the sale of screening rights to SKY and BT. The EPL remains able to attract capital as quickly as it spends it in the context of the wider economic recession due to a number of factors, including an increase in its customer base (as people seek relatively cheaper home-based entertainment), sponsors eager to win the battle to market their brands under more fierce competition from rivals and media corporations forced to increase bids to own the rights to live viewing to ward off competitors (the recent SKY bid increased partly due to pressure, perceived or otherwise, from Al Jazeera[32]). It would appear that the political economy of the EPL and so its short-term horizons have been seen as anathema to the progress of building the England's national team from a more enduring pool of talent.

Clearly, the obstacles placed on the development of the England national team by the EPL, considered here so far are important and cannot be ignored. Indeed, all the factors so far mentioned play a crucial role in explaining the culture of low expectations surrounding the England team at Euro 2012. However, whether taken separately or together, they cannot fully explain the culture of low expectations identified earlier. For one thing, the EPL has been in place since 1992, but the obstacles associated with the EPL we have outlined above have not, until now, had such a negative impact on *expectations* concerning the potential of the England team. The EPL and its commercializing imperatives were making their presence felt throughout the period of the 1990s and 2000s when our metaphorical 'hypergraph' moved so easily from boom to bust, from optimistic zeal to manic pessimism. Yet in 2012, it is very different: there is no boom and bust in emotions, meaning our hypothetical 'hypergraph' oscillates narrowly between 'no' to 'low expectations'. There must be other factors involved. It is worth considering the veracity of the view that 'The England football team [exemplifies a] collective delusion, and the country's rampant materialism ... ',[33] and so to what extent narratives surrounding the England team may still be in the grip of this same collective delusion in the very different context of neo-liberal-driven austerity.

The argument below suggests that the culture of 'low expectations' owes much to wider issues of national decline and renewal. To make this argument requires we stand back from the immediacies of the Euro 2012 setting and, having established this wider context, retrace our steps back to a firmer understanding of England 2012.

Football in the context of national decline

Wiener, the cultural historian of England's economic decline, remarked that, 'the more closely Britain's twentieth-century economic decline is examined, the more social and psychological elements are to be found entwined with economic factors'.[34] A thought echoed by Hobsbawm in relation to sport,

> What has made sport so uniquely effective as a medium for inculcating national feelings, at all events for males, is the ease with which even the least political or public

individuals can identify with the nation ... The imagined community of millions seems more real as a team of eleven named people'.[35]

As a 'medium for inculcating national feelings', the frequently analysed 'English decline thesis' presents itself as a discourse of renewal and decline (one cannot have a narrative of decline without its opposite – aspirations towards renewal) and has a certain resonance with the plight of the English national side. The thesis situates decline historically within a complex matrix of lack of economic productivity and cultural malaise, firstly within the rise and decline of Empire (late nineteent/early twentiethcentury) and then the rise and fall of the welfare state (post-1945–1980). The decline is positioned as a historical movement involving whole decades and requiring its opposite, aspirations towards renewal – the persistent hope/belief that decline can be halted and reversed. The rise of imperial dominance was based on the very forces that were claimed to be the cause of decline – the export of capital and financialization of the City of London.[36] Then, the loss of Imperial dominance rallied the forces of national economic planning and market regulation, calling forth hopes of a national economy framed within a welfare state and 'renewal within the commonwealth';[37] the perceived failure of the eventual culmination of national planning and market regulation – the welfare state – then became seen as the instrument of decline as renewal came forward in the guise of neo-liberalism.[38]

Within this complex and largely non-linear dialectic of decline and renewal, lies sport, particularly the national sentiment towards football. National identification with football offers a form of *soft power*,[39] an alternative battlefield, according to Beck, expressing to a global audience the continuing vitality of the nation, or, conversely, offering a platform for galvanizing woes about the wider fate of the nation.[40] This would appear to have been the case with regard to the national football team and the fate of the political economy in post-1945 Britain. The British political elite entered the 1950s, recently relegated from imperial supremacy by the USA, threatened by decolonization, over-shadowed by the Cold War, a partially complete welfare state and a population still limited to rationing their daily consumption needs. The British establishment had entered unknown terrain, reluctant to give up on ideas of global dominance and as yet unwilling to face the realities of a declining world power. The soft power of sport, in the form of the English national football team expressed this reluctance nowhere more clearly than in the two defeats Hungary inflicted, home and away.[41] The England team's fall from grace and well documented 6–3 thrashing at the hands of a brilliant Hungarian team at Wembley in November 1953, followed by a second defeat later in May 1954 'on the Danube', brought an avalanche of post-mortems in the national press, detecting manifestations of a serious malaise, concluding that 'the myth of England soccer supremacy has been shattered once and for all'.[42] Reflecting on further defeats in the mid 1950s at the hands of Yugoslavia, one *Guardian* reporter could perceive 'connections',

... between what was wrong with British football and what I felt increasingly to be wrong with British life as a whole. The traditional strength of the British has been the power to adapt themselves to changing conditions ... British improvisation has become slow and fumbling. At a time when her future depends entirely on making the most of her know-how, not only in industry but also in sport and the arts, she seems half-sunk in a complacent doze.[43]

Elective affinities between sporting and economic fortunes do wax and wane over time, but they are never too far from the surface. The dialectic of decline and renewal came to the fore again in the stagflationary 1970s. In hindsight, the UK economic recession during the 1970s proved to be the end of the political economy of Keynesianism as a means of establishing sustained capital expansion and halting longer term economic and political decline in the UK. Neo-liberalism (upon which the elite on the right of the political spectrum pinned their hopes of renewal) had by no means become dominant. The situation was one of transition, uncertainty, social pessimism and soul-searching as the elite looked for a way out of recession. The England national football team appeared to be infected by the same sense of atrophy, a harbinger for what was to come. At the beginning of the 1970s, the future looked rosy for England and a sense of optimism reigned among the football establishment. The England football team was being touted as a world force and favourite to retain the World Cup that year in Mexico. Despite eventually losing to West Germany in the quarter final of the World Cup, The 1970s England team was seen to be stronger and more gifted than the 1966 team that won in London and the media narrative around the England team remained relatively upbeat. Yet, by 1972 all sense of optimism had evaporated, the national side had fallen into disrepute and the manager, Sir Alf Ramsey, was holding on to his job at the whim of the FA, against mounting media pressure for wholesale changes to the England team setup. In the aftermath of a 1–1 draw against Poland at Wembley in November 1973, England failed to qualify for the 1974 World Cup, soon after Sir Alf Ramsey was dismissed as manager and England experienced an identity crisis as the reality of world mediocrity set in. As with England in 2011, the mood music for managerial appointments was far from optimistic. Brian Clough, manager of Derby County, claimed to have a clear vision of the necessary radical changes to be made, was judged unsuitable as the FA closed ranks, in favour of transitional figureheads, such as Joe Mercer, who came out of retirement to eventually become England's new caretaker manager. Mercer lasted 36 days in the Post, keeping it warm for the ill-fated reign of more traditional and austere Don Revie (the FA's preferred candidate), yet as Bagchi reflects, defeated once in 7 games, 'the reluctant caretaker did more than keep the house in order. He gave them a blueprint for renovation that was disastrously ignored when the caution and anxiety he had temporarily banished returned with a vengeance'.[44]

Clearly, the performance of the England team and how it is represented through the media expresses national concerns with the performance and fate of the national economy. How might this be expressing itself today in connection with the discourse of low expectations prevalent throughout the media? One answer I wish to pursue below is that the current narrative of 'low expectations' is expressive of deeper uncertainties regarding the larger political and economic canvas of neo-liberal renewal and more pertinently the growing awareness that neo-liberalism, so long glorified as the driving inspiration of consumerism, market freedom and globalization (all of which have engulfed the world of football and English football in particular), may be the source of malady and decline (as indeed, many have long claimed to know or suspect).

'Low expectations' in context: the decline of neo-liberalism

Since the global financial crisis hit the UK in 2008, commentators gradually began to realize that it had not also heralded the end of neo-liberalism as a way of organizing state and economy in ways that prioritized privatization and the freer rein of market principles. However, the crisis has not exactly revived neo-liberalism either. The reality is that neo-liberalism has lost credibility and lingers on in a political and economic vacuum. The neo-liberal project seems to be hanging on by the ironic twist of redefining 'progress' within a 'low expectations' economic and policy context. This is perhaps exemplified in the British coalition government's current economic policy, which, many have argued, is lacking in the imagination and courage necessary to come up with anything more than 'Plan A' as a means of 'renewal' in the face of a double-dip recession. The ironic twist is that this principal manifestation of 'renewal' looks very much like 'decline', given that it is currently based on data recording *cuts* (rather than growth) in public expenditure and merely signs of a slowdown in the rate of *contraction* of GDP growth per annum (not expansion). Such is the politics of austerity, the worry,

> ... is that low expectations risk *any* level of growth being seen as a vindication of the government's economic strategy. Some observers now talk of a new normal; they see low growth as something we just have to get used to ... [45]

> ... [w]e find ourselves in a ludicrous situation whereby the success or failure of the government's economic policy is being measured, by many, almost entirely in terms of whether we have two back-to-back quarters of negative growth or not.[46]

In the above quotes, 'low expectations' repositions (implodes) the difference between decline and renewal and would appear to echo the media repositioning of the English team from 'lame duck' to 'underdog' (a team who's 'renewal' comes to little more than the hope that they just might beat the odds by making do with respect to the players they have to hand and a fair wind at their back). In the topsy-turvy world of the broader neo-liberal crises within which cultures of sport find their expressions, 'growth forecasts' and 'growth outlooks sit side by side with evidence of economic contraction, until (so close is their proximity) they begin to stand in for each other as part of the dominant official discourses on the current major economic recession engulfing the UK,

> Britain's economy shrank less than first feared in the second quarter, but remains mired in the longest *double-dip recession* since the second world war ... The Treasury gave a *cautious welcome to the upward revision*, with a spokesman saying: 'Britain is dealing with some very deep-rooted problems at home and a very serious debt crisis abroad, and that is why the healing of the economy is proving to be a slow and difficult process. *Compared with two years ago, the deficit is down, inflation is down and there are more private sector jobs.*'[47]

As the above quote intimates, in a world observed through the prism of 'low expectations' the really bad news is often trumped by the 'good news', in this case we may be in a double dip recession, but at least the deficit is coming down and the Treasury can give a cautious welcome to any forecasting body predicting an 'upward revision'. Yet as The *Financial Times* indicates, The UK's double-dip recession has deepened sharply and unexpectedly, leaving the economy smaller than it was when the coalition government took office two years ago.[48]

This double-speak can be understood more readily if one examines the underlying commodity imperatives of the public/private, use value/exchange value contradictions underpinning the faltering neo-liberal project. In this respect, Harvey notes that in its heyday (post-Thatcher and throughout the Blair years) neo-liberal forms of capital accumulation focused on the privatization and deregulation of public institutions, leading to the hollowing out of their use value aspirations (public goods motivated by service to the community) for those more closely aligned with exchange value and the profit motive; the financialization of productive capital to the point where mergers, asset stripping and labour rationalizations became the preferred path; and consumer debt as a means of realizing the surplus value absorbed in commodities. This heyday responded to and hid a deeper problem of declining productivity of capital; defined by the average real growth in GDP across the EC, USA and Japan, the productivity of capital fell in oscillations from 6.5% in the 1960s to 1.8% in 2011.[49] The long-term decline in the productivity of capital, combined with the financialisation of the economy and public sector, set the seeds of neo-liberalism's economic swansong of low expectations in the form of the enormous global tsunami of surplus capital and labour. Global surplus of idle capital held by banks and financial institutions was valued at $61 trillion in 2008, a value almost double that of 2000 and over three times the value of world trade and in excess of global GDP in 2008.[50]

Against this backdrop, one can extrapolate that the current cul-de-sac facing neo-liberalism in the UK (in which 'Plan A' appears as the only plan) can be read along the lines that 'if exchange value and profits cannot flourish then neither can use value and by the same token if the market cannot flourish nor will the public sector'. In this respect, following Harvey, the deepening of the double-dip recession and the language of 'low expectations', invoked to manage our fears of the prospect of a deep recession, have their basis in a capital strike, which, as the double-dip recession intensifies, politicians appear virtually powerless to end.[51] The world is awash with surplus capital lying idle in global banks and financial institutions, in the face of the declining productivity of capital. Short of putting this major structural opposition back together, the UK government must plot a 'low expectations' ideology to manage expectations by 'revealing' growth prospects when they do not exist, or when they do exist promoting any growth figures as major sea-changes in the economy and/or signs of nationwide recovery.

It is reasonable to argue that the scale of the problem outlined by Harvey and the gap between it and the UK government's current policy of austerity are transferred via the media into 'low expectations' discourses that cross the political economic landscape attempting to manage expectations and hopes in the face of a major struc- tural crisis that governments can do relatively little about. It is this broader political economy that finds its expression within present day football. As we saw earlier, the discourse of 'low expectations' has refracted through the world of football and media representations of the England football team as it too is affected by the broader political economy, but also because it must manage expectations when faced by its own structural nemesis – the EPL. The two are fused in the minds of media pundits, as they reflect on the fate of the England team. As Conn points out, 'The Premier League, powered by intense sporting and commercial competition, provided perfect 'content' for the media during a consumer boom ... ', a 'perfect content' that came at the price of 'perfect discontent' when it came to the developmental aspira- tions of the English national team: 'The failure of the England team to improve is a visible consequence of a sport divided and confused about its purpose and priorities.

The national game was never reshaped with the England team at its apex, as the FA had wanted'.[52]

Conclusion

This paper set out to examine how the social binaries of public/market, lie at the heart of the narrative of 'low expectations' dominating media reportage of the England team in the run up to and during Euro 2012. What comes across clearly is the extent to which a discourse of 'low expectations' dominated media representations and the particular sub-plots of its domination. A number of salient reasons for this discourse have been outlined (including the barriers presented by the EPL), before centring on the influence of discourses operating in the wider political economy related to the economic crisis and how this is being played out in the UK. There is a clear elective affinity between media discourse on the national football team and the wider economy. This elective affinity becomes observable in the contrary aspirations of national team and EPL. In this sense, it has been shown that the discourse of 'low expectations', so pronounced in media representations, arises from both the wider economic context and the inter-mediate context between nation and club.

One the one hand, England's nemesis revolves around aspirations to produce a national team of enduring quality, which come up against and are trumped by the aspirations of the EPL, whose political economy towards football, fans and footballers, sets crushing limits to England's aspiration. One the other hand, as we have seen, the EPL is a necessary but not sufficient reason for the gloom surrounding the England team of late. This dubious 'honour', it has been argued, goes to the elective affinity between the new realism of low expectations within the wider political and cultural economy, which provides a wider context for understanding the language of low expectations saturating media narration of England's fate on the eve of and during the Euros. Media representations of the England team in previous tournaments managed to shrug off or conveniently forget about the structural barriers of the EPL, in the heat of national euphoria, not only during the events, but also in relation to the euphoria of consumerism and apparently unbridled economic growth and prosperity. The wider political and economic landscape is now one of uncertainty and transition, a place and space in which the language of decline and renewal have stalled and, in stalling, have collapsed into each other producing a culture of low expectations that finds its way into the football business sentiments regarding low expectations of the national side at Euro 2012.

Acknowledgement

I would like to express my thanks to Dr David Kennedy and Professor Hugh O Donnell for reading a first draft of this paper and providing such helpful comments.

Notes

1. Harvey, *The Enigma of Capital and the Crises of Capitalism*; Callinicos, *Contradictions of Austerity*, 65–77.
2. Giddens, 'The Third Way: The Renewal of Social Democracy'.
3. Wayne, 'Who Wants to be a Millionaire? Contextual Analysis and the Endgame of Public Service Television'.

4. England and monetary concerns are kept well apart: the subject of cash payment for putting on an England shirt is almost taboo, indicating that employment and performance is a matter of professional duty to a higher cause. The media's virtual silence of the millions of pounds recently spent on the English FA's new home for England, 'St George', is also testimony to issues of public good not market gain.
5. 'Scudamore argues that the breakneck climax to the season, with the league title and relegation issues going to the wire, had helped fuel the appetite for the Premier League "product"', in Gibson, 'Premier League Lands £3 billion TV Rights Bonanza from Sky and BT', June 13.
6. The term 'elective affinity' is one used by Max Weber in 1904 to explain the complex link between capitalism and religious beliefs and practices, in his major work, 'The Protestant Ethic and the Spirit of Capitalism', see Weber, *The Protestant Ethic and the Spirit of Capitalism*; and much more generally to understand how seemingly different relations, processes, events, develop in association with other seemingly different relations, processes and events in non-essential, but also non-accidental ways. The strength of the affinity is far from constant due to the intervening influences of other cross-cutting affinities. Contrary to much contemporary Marxism as economic reductivism, Marx had much more in common with Weber's view than some Marxists might suppose.
7. Mautner, 'The Entrepreneurial University', *Critical Discourse Analysis*, 100.
8. de Beear and Botha, 'News as Representation', in *Media Studies, Policy, Management and Media Representation*, ed. Fourie, 140.
9. See for e.g. Wodak and Meyer, *Methods of Critical Discourse Analysis*.
10. Wodak and Meyer, *Methods of Critical Discourse Analysis*, 5–6.
11. Vincente, *England Expects: English Newspapers' Narratives about the English Football Team in the 2006 World Cup*, 210.
12. Williams, 'England got what they Deserved – Absolutely Nichts'.
13. The Economist, *This England. The intertwined fates of a people and their football team*, Bagehot, June 10.
14. BBCSport, *World Cup 2010: BBC Sport asks who are the Champions?*, June 7.
15. Winwood, *Not-so-great Expectations: England go into Euro 2012 with a Notable Absentee – Hype'*, May 25.
16. BBCSport, *Euro 2012: Phil Jagielka Backs Roy Hodgson to Inspire England*, May 29.
17. Thinking Liberal, *Football: After Optimism Fails, England Fans Try Low Expectations*, June 10.
18. The Yorker (2012) 'Low expectations are the key to keeping England's hopes up', June 10.
19. Reuters UK, *Al Jazeera Sees Sporting Chance of Global Media Brand*, April 2, 2012.
20. Grandstand, *Euro 2012: Steely England keep France at Bay*, June 14.
21. Wilson, 'Euro 2012: How Refreshing – England for once does not Expect', May 19.
22. Press Conference – Hodgson, May 1.
23. McNulty, 'England Gamble on "Safe Option" Hodgson', April 29.
24. Burt, 'Roy Hodgson Interviewed for the England Manager's Job and Harry Redknapp Wishes him Well', April 30.
25. Bernstein, 'A Chairman David Bernstein Admits his Tenure will be Defined by Choosing Roy Hodgson as England Manager', May 1.
26. BBCSport, 'How will England do at Euro 2012?', May 30.
27. Neville, 'Gary Neville: England will not win Euro 2012', October 9.
28. Harwood, 'John Terry Race Row could Undermine England', October 27.
29. Bleacher Report, *England Football: Why do they Consistently Fail at Major Tournaments?*, April 18.
30. Bond, 'Priorities must Change for England to Succeed', June 25.
31. Conn, *Follow the Money*, August 30.
32. Reuters UK, *Al Jazeera Sees Sporting Chance of Global Media Brand'*, April 2.
33. The Economist, *This England. The intertwined fates of a people and their football team*, June 10.
34. Wiener, *English Culture and the Decline of the Industrial Spirit*, 3–4.
35. Hobsbawm, *Nations and Nationalism since 1780. Programme, Myth, Reality*, 143.

36. Gamble, 'Hegemony and Decline: Britain and the United States', in *Two Hegemonies: Britain 1846–1914 and the United States 1941–2001*, 127–140.
37. In particular the Sterling Area, binding dominions to the interests of British Imperial trade and finance, see Cain and Hopkins, 'Gentlemanly Capitalism and British Expansion Overseas II: New Imperialism, 1850–1945', 1–26.
38. Bacon and Eltis, *Britain's Economic Problem: Too Few Producers*.
39. Nye, *Soft Power: The Means to Success in World Politics*.
40. Beck, *Losing Prestige on and off the Field: England versus Hungary, 1953–1954*, 10–26.
41. See Note 40.
42. Fenier, *England could Never be Luckier, in Beck*, (2003): 14.
43. Dedijer, 'The Decline of English Football', 6.
44. Bagchi, 'The Forgotten Story of … England under Joe Mercer', October 11.
45. Weldon, 'A Weak Recovery isn't an Achievement', October 3.
46. Weldon, 'The Soft Bigotry of Low Expectations', April 3.
47. Kollewe, *UK GDP Revised Upwards – but Economy Remains in Double-dip*, August 24.
48. O'Connor and Cohen, *UK Economy Smaller than when Cameron Took Office*, July 25.
49. Foster and McChesney, *The Endless Crisis*, 1–30.
50. Roxburgh, et al. *Global Capital Markets: Entering a New Era*.
51. Harvey, *The Enigma of Capital and the Crises of Capitalism*.
52. Conn, *Follow the Money*, 25, 26.

References

Bacon, R., and W. Eltis. *Britain's Economic Problem: Too Few Producers*, (London: Macmillan, 1978).

Bagchi, R. 'The Forgotten Story of … England under Joe Mercer', *The Guardian*. http://www.guardian.co.uk/sport/blog/2012/oct/11/forgotten-story-joe-mercer-england-manager (accessed October 11, 2012).

BBCSport. *World Cup 2010: BBC Sport Asks who are the Champions?* http://news.-bbc.co.uk/sport1/hi/football/world_cup_2010/8716698.stm (accessed June 7, 2010).

BBCSport. *How will England do at Euro 2012?* http://www.bbc.co.uk/sport/0/football/18252657 (accessed May 30, 2012).

BBCSport. Euro 2012: *Phil Jagielka backs Roy Hodgson to Inspire England*. http://www.bbc.co.uk/sport/0/football/18251479 (accessed May 29, 2012).

Beck, P. 'Losing Prestige on and off the Field: England versus Hungary, 1953-4'. *Sport in History* 23, no. 2 (2003): 10–26.

Bernstein, D. 'A Chairman David Bernstein Admits his Tenure will be Defined by Choosing Roy Hodgson as England Manager'. *The Telegraph*. http://www.telegraph.co.uk/sport/football/teams/england/9239753/FA-chairman-David-Bernstein-admits-his-tenure-will-be-defined-by-choosing-Roy-Hodgson-as-England-manager.html (accessed May 1, 2012).

Bleacher Report. *England Football: Why Do they Consistently Fail at Major Tournaments?* http://bleacherreport.com/articles/646209-england-why-do-they-consistenly-fail-at-the-major-tournaments. (accessed April 18, 2011).

Bond, D. 'Priorities must Change for England to Succeed'. *BBC Sport*. http://www.bbc.co.uk/blogs/davidbond/2012/06/priorities_must_change_for_eng.html (accessed June 25, 2012).

Burt, J. 'Roy Hodgson Interviewed for the England Manager's Job and Harry Redknapp Wishes him Well, 2012'. *The Telegraph*. http://www.telegraph.co.uk/sport/football/teams/england/9236764/Roy-Hodgson-interviewed-for-the-England-managers-job-and-Harry-Redknapp-wishes-him-well.html (accessed April 30, 2012).

Callinicos, A. 'Contradictions of Austerity'. *Cambridge Journal of Economics* 36, no. 1 (2012): 65–77.

Conn, D. *Follow the Money*. http://www.lrb.co.uk/v34/n16/david-conn/follow-the-money (accessed August 30, 2012).

Dedijer, V. 'The Decline of English Football'. *The Guardian* (March 10, 1962): 6.

de Beear, A.S., and N. Botha. 'News as Representation'. In *Media Studies, Policy, Management and Media Representation*, ed. P.J. Fourie (vol. 2, 2nd ed.), 227–42. Cape Town: Juta 2007.

Fenier, B. 'England could never be luckier', Daily.\fimr, 22 Oct. 1953, cited in Beck, 'Losing Prestige on and off the Field: England versus Hungary, 1953-4'. *Sport in History* 23, no. 2 (2003): 10–26.

Foster, J.B., and R.W. McChesney. 'The Endless Crisis', *Monthly Review* 64 (May, 2012): 1–22.

Gamble, A. *'Hegemony and Decline: Britain and the United States', in Two Hegemonies: Britain 1846–1914 and the United States 1941–2001 Karl O'Brien and Armand Clesse*. Aldershot: Ashgate Publishing, 2002.

Gibson, O. 'Premier League Lands £3bn TV Rights Bonanza from Sky and BT'. *The Guardian*, June 13, 2012, http://www.theguardian.com/media/2012/jun/13/premier-league-tv-rights-3-billion-sky-bt (accessed June 14, 2012).

Grandstand, *Euro 2012: Steely England keep France at Bay*. http://www.stand-news.co.uk/sport/euro-2012-steely-england-keep-france-at-bay (accessed June 14, 2012).

Harvey, D. *The Enigma of Capital and the Crises of Capitalism*. London: Profile Books, 2010.

Harwood, J. 'John Terry Race Row could Undermine England'. *The Week*. http://www.theweek.co.uk/football/football-race-row/35727/john-terry-race-row-could-undermine-england#ixzz2A83ueUec

Hobsbawn, E.J. *Nations and Nationalism since 1780. Programme, Myth, Reality*. Cambridge: CUP, 1990.

Kollewe, J. *UK GDP Revised Upwards – but Economy Remains in Double-dip*. http://www.guardian.co.uk/business/2012/aug/24/uk-gdp-revised-economy-double-dip (accessed August 24, 2012).

Mautner, G. 'The Entrepreneurial University'. *Critical Discourse Analysis* 2, no. 2 (2005): 95–120.

McNulty, P. 'England Gamble on 'Safe Option' Hodgson'. *BBCSport*, http://www.bbc.co.uk/blogs/philmcnulty/2012/04/england_gamble_on_hodgson.html (accessed April 29, 2012).

Neville, G. 'Gary Neville: England will not win Euro 2012'. *The Telegraph* (2011). http://www.telegraph.co.uk/sport/football/teams/england/8816568/Gary-Neville-England-will-not-win-Euro-2012.html.

Nye, J.S. *Soft Power: The Means to Success in World Politics*. Aldershot: PublicAffairs, 2005.

O'Brien, Karl, and Clesse, Armand, eds. *Britain 1846–1914 and the United States 1941–2001* Aldershot: Ashgate Publishing, 2002.

O'Connor, S., and N. Cohen. 'UK Economy Smaller than when Cameron Took Office'. *FT*. http://www.ft.com/cms/s/0/4d4586da-d634-11e1-ba60-00144feabdc0.html#axzz29BNxRldT (accessed July 25, 2012).

Press Conference – Roy Hodgson. (May 1, 2012). http://www.thefa.com/video/England/Mens-Seniors/2012/belgium/press-conference – roy-hodgson.

Reuters UK. *Al Jazeera Sees Sporting Chance of Global Media Brand*. http://football.uk.reuters.com/leagues/champleague/news/2012/04/02/4A68DFFA-7CD6-11E1-A259-42358033923B.php (accessed April 2, 2012).

Reuters UK. *Hodgson's Job Helped by England's Low Expectations*. http://football.uk.reuters.com/leagues/champleague/news/2012/06/05/7D835F4C-AEAD-11E1-9CAF-07548033923B.php (accessed June 5, 2012).

Roxburgh, C., S. Lund, C. Atkins, S. Belot, Wayne W. Hu, and Moira S. Pierce. *Global Capital Markets: Entering a New Era*. Melbourne: Cinsey Global Institute, McKinsey and Company, September 2009.

The Economist This England. *The Intertwined Fates of a People and their Football Team, Bagehot*. http://www.economist.com/node/16317736 (accessed June 10, 2010).

The Yorker. *Low Expectations are the Key to Keeping England's Hopes Up*. http://www.theyorker.co.uk/sport/football/11637 (accessed June 10, 2012).

Thinking Liberal. *Football: After Optimism Fails, England Fans Try Low Expectations*. http://thinkingliberal.co.uk/?p=626 (accessed June 10, 2012).

Vincente, J., Edward M. Kian, Paul M. Pedersen, Aaron Kuntz, and John S. Hill. 'England Expects: English Newspapers' Narratives about the English Football Team in the 2006 World Cup'. *International Review for the Sociology of Sport* 45, no. 2 (2010): 199–223.

Wayne, M. 'Who wants to be a Millionaire? Contextual Analysis and the Endgame of Public Service Television', in *Formations: 21st Century Media Studies*, ed. D. Fleming, 196–201. Manchester: MUP, 2000.

Weber, M. *The Protestant Ethic and the Spirit of Capitalism*. New York: Dover Publications, 2003.

Weldon, D. 'The Soft Bigotry of Low Expectations'. *Touchstone*. http://touchstoneblog. org.uk/2012/04/the-soft-bigotry-of-low-growth-expectations/ (accessed April 3, 2012).

Weldon, D. 'A Weak Recovery isn't an Achievement', *Touchstone*. http://touchstoneblog. org.uk/2012/10/a-weak-recovery-isnt-an-achievement/ (accessed October 3, 2012).

Wiener, M.J. *English Culture and the Decline of the Industrial Spirit 1850–1980* (Middlesex: Penguin Books, 1981), 3–4.

Williams, R.'England got What they Deserved – Absolutely Nichts'. *The Guardian*. http:// blogs.guardian.co.uk/worldcup06/2006/07/03/england_got_what_they_deserved.html (accessed July 6, 2006).

Wilson, P. 'Euro 2012: How Refreshing – England for once does not Expect', *The Guardian* (May 19, 2012).

Winwood, I. *Not-so-great Expectations: England go into Euro 2012 with a Notable Absentee – hype*. http://www.mirror.co.uk/sport/football/euro-2012-why-low-expectations-make-847297 (accessed May 25, 2012).

Wodak, R., and M. Meyer. *Methods of Critical Discourse Analysis*. London: Sage, 2009.

Index

For Product Safety Concerns and Information please contact our EU
representative GPSR@taylorandfrancis.com Taylor & Francis Verlag GmbH,
Kaufingerstraße 24, 80331 München, Germany

Batch number: 08153807

Printed by Printforce, the Netherlands